L

MARGARET POWELL'S LONDON SEASON

UNABRIDGED

PAN BOOKS : LONDON

First published 1971 by Peter Davies Ltd
This edition published 1973 by Pan Books Ltd,
33 Tothill Street, London SW1

ISBN 0 330 23596 6

Printed in Great Britain by
Richard Clay (The Chaucer Press), Ltd, Bungay, Suffolk

To my escort Leigh (Reggie) Crutchley who,
though he behaved with a complete lack of chivalry
throughout my Season, nevertheless gave me
a whale of a time.

CONTENTS

INTRODUCTION

As all I knew about the London Season sprang from when I was in service, I looked upon doing it with a somewhat jaundiced eye. It had seemed to me that the people who did the Season were so far removed from ordinary mortals as not to be credible. Perhaps it was like that in the Twenties. I'd imagined it as a kind of marriage market for the young ladies of the nobility, the upper classes. I still think that in those days the Season was not so much a luxury as a necessity, because it was practically the only chance that that kind of young woman had to see and be seen, except in her home where she had, like any of us, to be seen and not heard.

I was also apprehensive because I knew it would mean me moving amongst people of a different class; people doing the Season because it was the Thing their kind of people did by tradition. I knew I would be an outsider, and a rank outsider at that, so I expected to be treated as one and cold-shouldered out of any possible enjoyment. I wasn't.

It seems to me that people are far more democratic than they used to be in the old days. I can't imagine that when I was below stairs the kind of people who were doing the Season then would ever have allowed themselves to tell me the time of day, let alone chat with me and be as friendly with me as they would have been with one of their own class.

Sometimes I couldn't help thinking that this breaking

down of the classes had not been a pulling up by the boot-straps of the lower classes to the upper, but a levelling down of everybody so that we're all a sort of mediocre mass. Or is it that I expected from the gentry a higher standard of intelligence and intelligent observation and conversation than I got?

Being a woman I was a bit worried about clothes. All right, through making television appearances and going around speaking at meetings and such like I've increased my wardrobe but it's not that extensive. However, with a little dress sense and a lot of ingenuity it's amazing how often you can ring the changes. You can appear to be in something different while you still use the main thing – it's just that you team it up with different accessories so that you give the impression you're wearing different clothes for each occasion.

While many of the events of the Season are by men and for men and were originally used as a sort of cockerel's display to show men off to women, women have I think very largely taken over. They provide the light relief, sometimes the only real entertainment.

I just can't imagine Henley without the women – I know they don't row, and I'm very glad they don't. It would be most undignified for them to be seen sliding along on their backsides, but their presence there takes away from the incongruity of the men doing it. The women grace every event. I don't think half the men would go if it wasn't for them.

But although particularly for the debutantes the Season has lost its original purpose, it has gained in other ways. There's lots of fun to be had and plenty to be learnt from it. I hope that even when I seem to criticize, you will understand that I very much enjoyed my London Season.

QUEEN CHARLOTTE'S BALL

I ONCE went as a daily for an elderly gentleman who often used to take up my time relating the exploits of his youth. There was nobody else for him to talk to, but I was still flattered that he conversed with his daily at all. In particular, he'd tell about the places he'd been to, the famous events he'd attended and the well-known people he'd met. Talk about name-dropping – he place-dropped as well. As he seemed a person of no particular social or financial significance, I used to wonder how he got invited to all the functions. Eventually I asked him.

'Good heavens,' he said, 'I wasn't invited. There were half a dozen of us who had just left Oxford with time on our hands and no money, so we formed a sort of club called The Unauthorized Enterers. It sounded more elegant than The Gatecrashers, but that's what we were. It was largely a matter of self-assurance, and since we were all fairly good-looking we'd plenty of that. We perfected it to a fine art and were rarely asked to leave.'

I thought how dashing and adventurous they all must have been and what fun they must have had. But I never dreamed that one day I, too, would be an Unauthorized Enterer at one of the most important events of the London Season, Queen Charlotte's Ball.

Never in a million years would I have thought of gate-crashing, nor would I have agreed to it if I'd known about it beforehand. I was expecting to be driven up to Grosvenor House and ushered in in style. However, according to my escort, although no stone had been left unturned, and people had been digging around until the very last minute, permission for us to observe the proceedings even from the balcony had been refused.

I was all set to make tracks for home and I told him so. 'No,' he said, 'don't do that, we'll get in all right – just leave it to me. We should worry – I've been thrown out of better places than Grosvenor House.' Not a remark calculated to fill me with confidence or enthusiasm. As I wavered he followed this up with, 'Come and have a drink.' I knew then I was sunk. Once behind a glass I'd be persuaded into any nefarious undertaking – well, almost any.

'Now this is the plan,' he began after he'd brought me a large whisky. 'I've had an opportunity of casing the joint.' Casing the joint! I was already feeling like a criminal without him talking like one; and calling Grosvenor House a 'joint' struck me as sacrilege. 'There's a way up to the balcony which looks on to the ballroom,' he went on, 'and if we get there around the time that the debs are preparing to troop down to their cake, everyone will be so preoccupied with them we can slip in without being noticed.' The way he said it made it sound easy, or perhaps it was the scotch doing its work.

'I'll lead the way,' he went on, 'and you'll follow carrying my briefcase, looking as if you're my secretary. Whatever happens, don't speak; that would be disastrous. You might manage to look like a secretary, but you couldn't sound like one in a million years!' He must have noticed the expression on my face because he hastily said, 'It's all right – once you're inside you can talk your head off. Now' – he checked his watch – 'let's forget all about it for a couple of hours.'

In the event, he was quite right. His tactics worked and the timing was impeccable. We took a taxi to the main entrance of Grosvenor House, then swept in through the swing doors with him steaming ahead. I couldn't see his face but his behind was very purposeful. He weaved along through what looked to me like a stately collection of the upper crust. Only once did we seem in any danger and that was when someone in uniform made as if he was going to question our presence. Before he could utter, my escort called out, 'Ballroom Gallery?' as though he was inquiring for the platform of the ten o'clock train to Brighton. 'Straight on, sir,' came the reply, and we ploughed forward. I don't know what I looked like, but I know I felt horrible. All I could think about was keeping my mouth shut and I clamped my lips so tight together that my jaws ached.

At last we were safely in the gallery. We sat hidden behind a pillar and took stock of the situation. I unbuttoned my coat and worked my mouth up and down to get rid of my lock-jaw. My escort was smiling. As I started to take off my coat his expression changed.

'Oh, my gawd,' he groaned, 'look at your frock!'

'What's the matter with it?'

'Relate it to the surroundings,' he said.

I did and I didn't like what I saw. I'd thought that as we were going to be among young people I'd try and be with it, so I'd put on a psychedelic dress. Talk about sticking out like a sore thumb!

I went on the defensive. 'It won't notice too much,' I said.

'Won't notice! You'd stand out two miles in a London smog!'

With that he went off to get some drinks, and I had a chance to take a look at the floor below.

The true purpose of Queen Charlotte's Ball is to raise money for Queen Charlotte's Hospital. It's been doing this since 1925. The money provides extra comforts and

13

amenities for patients and staff, and is also put towards financing research and buying equipment. The contributions made by the National Health Service wouldn't be enough for all that is done there and the money raised by the Ball certainly helps. But as I looked down at the whole scene and thought of the expense of staging the Ball – the hire of the ballroom, the dinner, the band, the thousands of pounds spent on dresses – I couldn't help feeling that if all that had been given to the hospital direct it would amount to many times what the Ball would raise. But I suppose people don't give like that; they want something for their money. Well, what were they getting?

From my position in the gallery the present scene was not particularly remarkable. We'd arrived at that sort of limbo period in any dinner-dance. The meal was over; the men were cradling their brandies; the women were either chattering away in little groups or retiring to repair the damage that eating a meal does to faces; and the band was getting ready for the dancing which was to follow. There was only one feature which made the picture different from others of its kind; all the young girls, the debutantes, were wearing long white dresses. This is the custom and the rule at Queen Charlotte's Ball.

I suppose some word must have been whispered around, because suddenly I noticed that all the debs were making their way to the gallery, where they formed up in ranks. When the ballroom had lost its last piece of whiteness, there was a fanfare from the band heralding what was for me the really impressive event of the evening. It was the descent of the debs down the broad staircase, on to the ballroom floor. I'd got more confidence by now, so I stood by the railings of the gallery and watched the girls as they passed by. Obviously the whole thing had been rehearsed; I understand this is done the same morning and, give them their due, they put on a very good show. The expressions on their faces were interesting. Some looked bored – or perhaps, as they concentrated, their faces fell into a bored expression; others giggled nervously like naughty choirboys; some had glazed eyes and a slight wobble (and I knew what that meant); while others, either to the manner born or as a result of some training as models, sailed or wafted down the staircase. When they got to the bottom they peeled off in pairs around a huge iced cake, lit with what seemed to be hundreds of electric candles and standing on something that looked for all the world like the thing a coffin's wheeled off the hearse on. It was of course decoratively covered in linen. Then, when they were assembled on the ballroom floor, the girls and cake advanced up the room. I glanced at the faces of the mums, dads or chaperones at the tables on either side of the ballroom. While the mums mostly seemed to have harrassed expressions on their faces and looked much more worried than their daughters, the dads' eyes were definitely twinkling at either their own daughters or somebody else's. Though a few, I thought, might be thinking what it had cost them and were a bit unsure as to whether it was worth it.

When the procession reached the other end of the ballroom the girls stopped and, at a given signal, dropped down in a curtsy to the Duchess of Northumberland. So the annual ritual had once again been observed.

One thing that amazed me was how 150 girls in white could all look different, even if the difference was small. Some of the dresses reminded me of my young dancing days, when we wore tight bodices and rows and rows of frills. There were a few trouser-suits with almost full-length tunics, but they were not as effective as the dresses. It's very difficult to wear white – you walk a tightrope between looking like a bride, being dressed for your

Confirmation, or just about to retire for the night. One or two girls, with either no mother to guide them or a determination to wear what they fancied, were in shiny white satin. A grave error, unless one is very slim at the rear.

White also makes a girl look defenceless. This may have pleased the young men around, but before I had a chance of talking to the debs, I at any rate almost felt sorry for them. I thought, This is it, girls. You've been protected by your schools, colleges and finishing-schools. Now you're launched. Your mothers and fathers have done everything they can for you. Now they've put you out to sea to sail for a matrimonial port and may the journey there be a smooth one.

I felt the parents were treating their daughters as if they were some elaborate delectable dish that had taken hours to prepare and contained all the most expensive ingredients, and were now standing back in pride and admiring the finished product. A dish fit for a king, they were murmuring. And while they were probably not aiming quite so high, you may be sure they wanted them consumed or consummated by someone near that class bracket. Mind you – let's face it – whether parents are well off or not, they want their daughters to make the best possible marriage. They may say they are content for them to be in love; on the other hand they do their best to make sure that they mix in the kind of circles where love and money go together.

Later I asked one of the girls if she would be keeping her white dress until she got married, only to be answered with a hoot of laughter. 'You must be joking – I wouldn't be seen dead in this again! If and when I get hitched, I shall wear the proper gear, not this fancy dress!' I don't know what she meant by 'proper gear', I thought that white dresses *were* the proper clothes for a bride.

By now the cake was being handed round, just like at a wedding. There was some controversy as to whether it was real icing on the outside, or just covered by a cardboard container. When I saw it with all those electric candles on, I was sure that it couldn't be real because the heat would have melted it. With a little tactful research, I found out I was right. The cake was in a container and weighed 200 lb. Judging by the speed with which people were being served, much of it must have already been in slices. I was shown a piece and it certainly looked a lovely rich, dark texture. I wouldn't have minded a slice of it myself, but, as a gatecrasher, my hopes of getting one were remote indeed.

The men's dress – or should I call it 'gear'? – was assorted. I'd expected to see them all in tails, but generally it was only the older men who wore them; the younger ones were in dinner jackets. I wonder why most men look so dignified and impressive wearing tails because, really, when it's examined objectively, it's a ridiculous outfit: an expanse of cloth split up the middle, which makes so many of the shorter men look, from the back view, like penguins. And the action when they flick them up before sitting down is ridiculous, if not downright vulgar. One young man obviously fancied himself as a Regency buck. He was wearing a long, plum-coloured tunic edged with gold braid and a sporty-looking cravat. Some of the others were almost as pretty as the girls; they certainly appeared to have spent just as much time at the hairdresser's. This unisex look seemed to have confused other people besides me, for I saw one young man come up and kiss another young man! I couldn't help wondering what I'd have done if I'd seen that when I was a girl and men were in such short supply.

By now, psychedelic dress or not, I began mixing with people and got talking to a few ex-debs who were acting as chaperones. Some of them looked more attractive than their charges – perhaps, since they'd already been through the mill, they felt more assured. One of them said she preferred being a chaperone because she was getting all the pleasures of the Ball without the apprehension. She hadn't got to worry whether she had made the right entrance, whether her dress was right, whether there was another one exactly like it, was her escort bored with her, was she making the right kind of impression; she could just sit back and enjoy it. In lots of ways it's like going to another person's wedding shortly after you've been married yourself. You've lots of worries at your own wedding, wondering whether you look all right, are the cars going to arrive, is Mum going to cry, is the bridegroom going to turn up, will Uncle get blind drunk at the reception and tell his foul stories; but, once you've done it all, and you're just an onlooker and a critic at someone else's, you get the pleasures without the worries.

I thought that there might be a heavy sense of responsibility in chaperoning. But one, an elder sister, though only by two years, admitted she felt none. 'In any case,' she said, 'it makes no difference what I say, she does what she wants.'

'Why have a chaperone, then?' I asked.

'It's the done thing. Although they come with an escort, they're all expected to have one.'

I suppose it makes sense, but I couldn't see it. However, as I say, she was having herself a ball. She had a permanent young man and was shortly to get married, and she didn't have to worry whether she was giving a return for all that had been spent on her.

I was curious to know how the debutantes got invited to the Ball. Each year it is advertised in the Personal Column of *The Times*, and applications are invited for tickets, which cost seven guineas each, or did for this year.

Anyone, of course, can apply for tickets, but in practice it's like Heaven – few are chosen. During the evening I asked around as to how the selection was made, but no one could give me a firm answer. The nearest I got was, 'You're either on the list or you're not.' I was to hear often enough about this mysterious 'list', but I never did learn how it was compiled.

I did have a passing thought, that to make it look as if they were operating in a democracy, the organizers could have given a few free places at the Ball to ordinary working-class girls. But no, on reflection I dismissed it because that would mean their mums and dads coming with them. And I couldn't see them fitting in.

It was the same with the escorts. I said to one deb, 'Suppose you were one of those off-beat girls and would like the milkman or a bus conductor as your escort, would you be allowed to bring him?'

'Good heavens, no!' she replied. 'It couldn't happen. In any case, he wouldn't feel comfortable here.'

I couldn't see why as I looked down on the ballroom. To me it looked much the same as a *palais de danse*, only in a more opulent setting. There they all were, jigging away on the dance floor, rocking and jiving and giving the usual imitations of suffering from St Vitus' Dance, none of which seemed to go with long white dresses and tails.

By now the gallery was getting pretty crowded with the debs and their boyfriends, because the bar was up there, and, to contradict what the deb had said to me about working-class escorts feeling out of place, I was astonished at the number of people who seemed to want to talk to me. After all, there was I, a Cockney ex-char who'd gate-crashed into what I thought they would regard as their sacred precincts and they weren't sending me up, they were sending themselves and the occasion sky high. They left me with the feeling that the organizers are out of touch with the modern young scene, and that Queen Charlotte's is not for the debs at all – it's run for the sake of the parents and organizers.

Another of my earlier illusions to be shattered was my conviction that with young men just having left their public schools or universities mixing with well-educated girls, there would be a lot of intellectual to-ing and fro-ing. But, no, it was the same old drivel that I heard at the dances in my youth. 'Isn't it hot?' – 'Lovely floor' – 'Have you seen so-and-so?' Same old stuff, only delivered in a different accent. We'd been joined now by a group of these young escorts. They all seemed to have one eye on the ballroom, and I might have known, like any gathering of men they were discussing and comparing the sexual merits or demerits of the debs.

To my embarrassment my escort encouraged them, though he apologized afterwards, saying it was in the cause of research. I'd always thought that ladies weren't discussed in the Mess and I'd supposed that meant a wider context than the Services. Yet here were these young men making the most scandalous remarks, even accusing some of the girls of smoking pot.

I sprang to the defence of my sex: 'Balderdash! You're just saying all this to impress me. Well, it doesn't. I know my own sex and you can say what you like, they haven't changed that much since I was a girl!' 'Have it your own way, dahling – think what you like,' was the supercilious reply.

I must say it's impossible to argue with this kind of young man, but I got the conversation rolling again nevertheless. 'In spite of what you say, looking at those girls all in white, there's something aesthetic, a feeling of beauty, youth, and purity.'

I realized as I said it that I should have left that purity

bit out. 'Pure!' They howled with laughter. 'Fifty per cent of them are on the pill – and only ten per cent are doing it more in hope than anticipation. The Season will decimate virginity.'

I was getting exasperated. 'Don't you reckon to take a girl out for an evening and just kiss her goodnight afterwards and leave it at that?'

'Good heavens, you can't find girls like that nowadays! If you were just to kiss a girl goodnight, she would think you were drunk or queer!'

I still don't believe it. I don't believe that girls are all like that. I know you read in the papers about the Permissive Society, but I refuse to believe that there aren't as many nice girls nowadays that are prepared to go out, have a good evening and just say goodnight. Not every evening, surely, ends up in bed! How could they stand the pace?

I looked at the weedy Etonian who was doing most of the talking. There he was in a tail suit and scruffy shirt, with a bit of red chiffon knotted under his chin – I wouldn't have given him house room in the old days, even when there was a shortage of men. All right, I used to say, any port in a storm; but debs today can't find it as stormy as that!

By now I was sick of this one-track conversation, so I again tried to shift ground. What, I asked one, was he going to do now that he'd left Eton? 'I have joined the mass of unemployed,' he said. 'There is my bread until September,' and he gestured to the ballroom. 'I shall be asked to the debs' dances, because there's always a shortage of young men, and those I'm not invited to I, like you, will gatecrash. I shall have all the dollies I want and all the food I can consume at parties; drink will flow there too; and what extra I need I shall swipe. I shall live comfortably!'

Looking back on this particular part of the evening, I like to think that perhaps there was a lot of micky-taking going on. That they looked on me as an inquisitive old busybody and thought that they might as well give me something to write about. Well they did and I have, but it's probably best taken with a pinch or even a handful of salt.

We were joined now by a party of debs and the conversation switched to where they were all going on to after the Ball. It seemed that a nightclub called 'Annabel's' was to everybody's taste and they got ready to leave.

Shortly after this, to my surprise, I heard the National Anthem being played. Like Cinderella, I couldn't believe the time had passed so quickly. I must say I'd enjoyed myself hugely even though I'd not had a dance. The ballroom started to clear rapidly. My escort hustled me out the same way as we had come in.

No Annabel's for us – we settled for an all-night café, where we ruminated on an exhilarating evening.

It seemed to me that as far as the debs were concerned, Queen Charlotte's had given them a social *cachet* – they could now feel that they were Somebodies. They were, perhaps, not wildly excited about it, but it was the start of the Season and meant that they would get invited to many other dances and social events during it.

The young men were more blasé. It wasn't their kind of thing, I imagine, because they were very much playing second fiddle. They professed that they didn't have to worry about future invitations. 'The number of available, eligible men is limited,' one had said, 'so I should have been asked everywhere whether I'd been here to-night or not.'

I was surprised at the number of debs who thought it a good thing to preserve the tradition. Their only regret was they were no longer presented at Court. They disliked the more democratic tendencies of today. Such things as the Royal walkabouts in Australia were to them a great mistake. They made the Queen seem an ordinary person, and 'you can't look up to an ordinary person, can you?'

They were pleasant, likeable girls, but I felt that they wished to preserve certain functions and an area of society which was theirs and theirs alone. After all, there has to be some point to having money and position?

My escort was elated about his part in the whole affair. 'An excellent plan brilliantly carried out,' he said, with some pride. 'Nobody any the wiser. We must see the publishers in the morning and let them into the secret.'

We could have saved ourselves that journey. They already knew. The William Hickey column in the *Daily Express* carried the story about our gatecrashing.

I haven't worn that psychedelic dress since.

THE WINDSOR HORSE SHOW

GROSVENOR HOUSE, Park Lane, isn't far geographically from the Windsor Horse Show, but the events in every other way are poles apart. At Queen Charlotte's Ball, all was light, music, gaiety and warmth. At Windsor it was grey, wet and cold, with an intensity of purpose among both horses and riders that made it an occasion only for enthusiasts. I was definitely not an enthusiast and I hoped that the Season would not have many other such ordeals for me. Although I'd been assured that the Show was very much a part of the London Season, I couldn't see the gay butterflies that had danced at the Ball surviving the Arctic conditions that were prevailing.

Between Staines and Windsor my escort and I stopped at a pub on the banks of the River Thames. It was called The Bells of Ouzley. I like most pubs at any time, but some I like more than others. Immediately we got inside I knew this one would be high on my list. The beer was splendid. The unusual name derives from the reign of Henry VIII. He, in a rage because his matrimonial intentions were not approved by the Church, decided that all monasteries were a drug in the market. So they were abolished. For some reason or another the monks from the monastery of a place called Ouzley were very partial to their bells, so they put them in boats and ferried them down the river, eventually burying them near where this Inn now is. What use the bells were without anywhere for them to ring, I don't know – it's not my problem – nor is there any evidence that they were ever dug up again, so their labours were in vain except that they gave the name to this pub. Mind you, it's probably legend just as so many of the exploits more directly attributed to Henry VIII are, otherwise he would have had a very busy and exhausting life!

Incidentally, a character in one of my favourite books, *Three Men in a Boat*, also approved of the beer at The Bells of Ouzley, so if Harris liked it, then it was certainly good enough for me! As I was inquiring about its history I was surprised to find that Queen Elizabeth I hadn't slept there. It must be one of the few places where she didn't.

We enjoyed the drink and company so much we decided to stay to eat. We hadn't time to try the restaurant so we lunched at The Captain's Table, a cold-buffet bar, and it was excellent. When we'd finished the meal I was ready to face anything – even the Windsor Horse Show.

I've only ever ridden once, bareback on an enormous shire horse. I was about eight or nine at the time. It seemed like sitting on a mountain; directly it started to jog along, I fell off. However, in my youth horses were a source of income. With my brothers I used to go out in the streets collecting their droppings and selling manure by the bucketful so that we could augment our ha'penny-a-week pocket money. Apart from that, all I know about horses is that the ones I put my money on never run fast enough. Mind you, I prefer horses to dogs. I know that you can't train horses to fetch your slippers or carry your newspaper, but then, who wants to? At least with horses I don't have to keep throwing buckets of water down the pavement.

Getting to the Show presented no problems. The roads were signposted and there were plenty of car parks. It was the journey from our car to the Members' Enclosure that was the hazard. The rain had turned the approaches into a skid pan and I slewed from side to side like a drunken sailor. Once inside the ground we staggered along through what might have been my idea of an oriental bazaar except that the goods on display were all to do with horses and their riders – not things that were likely to have aroused my interest even if I could have concentrated on anything except trying to keep on my feet.

Eventually we reached the enclosure, and I sat gratefully on a canvas chair – after first making sure that it was firmly fixed (I'm always rather apprehensive of canvas chairs ever since one collapsed under me just as I was doing my best to convince a new boyfriend that in me he would have a treasure). When I'd got my breath back I looked round and was disappointed in what I saw. I had expected that the Windsor Horse Show might be a bit like a race-meeting – after the style of Ascot, where people parade in between the events wearing fashionable clothes, with the debs and their escorts being a bit *bizarre* in their dress. It was nothing like that at all! Everyone seemed sort of 'country-looking', with their tweedy clothes, ancient hats or scarves tied under the chin, and sensible brogues – the country gentry, in fact. They seemed impervious to the foul weather.

We were sitting in the fourth row. We could have got nearer, but I reckoned that if any of the horses got frisky the people in front would provide us some protection. Under ordinary circumstances we'd have been able to see everything that went on but every time it rained, up went umbrellas. So the view we got was through the spikes of these umbrellas and we also had the discomfort of the drips landing on to our legs. Still, by now I was so uncomfortable that a few extra irritations didn't really make much difference!

It was Royal Windsor's Twenty-seventh Year and it

seemed to me that probably the same people had been going ever since it started. I've got to admit it, the British have stamina if they've got nothing else!

We'd arrived when what is the most popular part of any horse show was in progress; the jumping. The object was to jump the poles, walls, gates and fences cleanly, without knocking anything over, and to do a clear round in the fastest time. Well, for a couple of rounds or so this interested me, and I have to admit that it was thrilling at first to see the way the horses jumped so gracefully over a five-barred gate. I even shut my eyes once or twice, I was sure the rider would be catapulted off. But soon the monotony of it got me down, the excitement wore off. I'd been hoping for the fun of the fair, with people yelling at the tops of their lungs urging on the horse that they fancied. Instead, it was like a school prize-giving, just polite little clapping, and the same claps whether the horse did well or not. The spectators' attitude was like that of the man who gives the prizes away. He shakes hands with those who have won and then congratulates all those who haven't for being jolly good losers.

One thing that I was happy to see, as an ardent feminist, was the women competing successfully with the men. It was difficult to make out how young or attractive they were, though, because they were all wearing the same clothes. This I think is a pity. Why can't they look more feminine? I know they've got to wear breeches and boots, but so do a lot of women who don't even have to. These could be more colourful and they could really go to town on their shirts and jackets. Their caps too could certainly be made to do something for them. It would liven things up a bit and might attract the crowds. After all, they could go to town on their clothes a lot more than the women tennis players do at Wimbledon, and look at the sensation they create each year! Who knows, it might even make the spectators do something about themselves.

It's always surprised me that they don't allow women to ride as jockeys at race-meetings. I can see no reason why they couldn't do as well as men. One thing, they wouldn't have the weight problem that men have. Dieting would come naturally to them. Some women would, of course; Tessie O'Shea would have to starve before she could get on a horse! Then, like me, she probably doesn't want to.

This particular competition seemed endless to me. It was like some time-honoured ritual to be performed: nobody knows why, they only know it is the thing to do. All was quietness and decorum. The watchers seemed entranced by the scene; their facial expressions never changed.

An elderly and well-bred couple, sitting just in front of us, were an exception; they did show some expression but in a peculiar place. They leaned forward intently on their seats as each competitor entered the ring. There was a sort of tension in their backs as horse and rider approached each obstacle. Then, up they would rise together, off their chairs in unison with the rider, before plonking back with an expression of relief if the fence was cleared, or a twinge of disgust if it wasn't. I was fascinated by them. I didn't bother to watch the ring. Looking at this backside commentary, I knew exactly what was going on. By the end of the afternoon I reckon those two must have been completely exhausted. But I'd learnt something. I'd always thought the toast 'Bottoms up' rather vulgar – I see now what it means and that its derivation is an aristocratic one.

To me the high spot of the Show was the Trade Horse Competition. I think this was because I felt that, like me, they were an alien breed amongst such equine aristocracy. Those shire horses combined good looks with utility, like the country peasants of Old England. At that moment I envied them the long hair round their ankles which made it look from a distance as though they were wearing fur gaiters. My freezing feet could have done with a pair. Part of my enthusiasm for this event could be due to the fact that they were mostly pulling Brewers' Drays – a sort of association of ideas.

But I've always liked working horses. I used to be proud of my husband Albert's horse that pulled his milk-float. When I saw them both trotting down the street I was reminded of Ben Hur and his chariot. In fact Ben Hur had nothing on Albert at that time. Unfortunately, what I didn't realize was that Albert wouldn't always look like Ben Hur after we were married. Besides, there was no room to park the chariot at home. When Albert went to work as a furniture remover after the war, his firm had put a team of four horses to pull one of their trucks. Like those at Windsor, they were mostly used for advertisement and show purposes, though they did do some jobs. In fact some of the firm's customers used to insist on having the horses to move their furniture.

It was noticeable that these more plebeian horses had most plebeian habits. They answered the call of nature when and where it pleased them. All my childhood instincts rose to the fore and I wished I could rush into the ring with a bucket. I was reminded of Sir Beerbohm Tree's remark when a similar thing happened with an animal on the stage of his theatre. 'Ah,' he said, 'not only an actor but a critic.'

During this display I noticed that one of the shire horses, every time he passed the judges, seemed to change his kind of step from clod-hopping to prancing as delicately as a ballet dancer. It was as if he knew that it was there he was to be judged. I wondered if the driver gave him a secret signal or if the horse had the sense to know he was on show. Either way it showed a remarkable intelligence.

After this event it was back to the jumping in which I had now lost interest, so I turned over the pages of my programme. I came to a list of the charities which benefit from the Show. I was interested that last year the Windsor and District Moral Welfare got £420 as against the Old People's Welfare £100. Things haven't changed much in some people's minds since I was in service when I found that people were more concerned over my morals than they were over my physical welfare. I know that one doesn't need to worry about morals of the old people but I could wish that more was done for their comfort.

Eventually my escort suggested that we had tea. I agreed with alacrity, and we made for the nearby marquee. Since I seem to have gone on a bit about the events, let me say that the catering was excellently done.

You do, as I've said, need to be a dedicated lover of horseflesh to spend an afternoon watching the same thing over and over again, with a cold wind reddening your nose and rain ruining your hairstyle. It was the most uneventful event I had ever been to in my life. If only someone had sworn at their horse, shouted 'Foul', abused the judges, or given some show of excitement, I'd have been happier. But then nobody would. Anything so sordid couldn't have happened in that rarefied old sheepdog atmosphere!

THE CHELSEA FLOWER SHOW

THE Great Spring Show was begun by The Royal Horticultural Society in 1888. It didn't have a very propitious
start, since records show that on May 17th–18th of that
year it rained almost solidly. However, gardeners in this
country are made of stern stuff – they have to be – so the
Show has continued ever since, the only interruption
being the years of the two world wars.

It is still held in May. I wondered why that month was
chosen because even with my limited knowledge I know
that few plants are in bloom in the ordinary garden. Apparently May was decided on because many of the gentry
left their London houses for the country in June, and
since their flowers were mostly all grown in glasshouses
and conservatories it didn't make any difference to them.
Like me you may well ask why in more democratic times
the date hasn't been moved forward. Well this is Britain,
isn't it?

I'm not what you would call a lover of plants or
flowers. I think they're very nice growing in the ground. I
notice them but they don't interest me, which is just as
well because whereas some people have green fingers I've
got lethal fingers – every plant I touch withers away.

I did try gardening for a short time but I speedily gave
up, especially as our minute front garden was a haven for
all the insects in creation. Furthermore, as soon as I'd
nearly broken my back digging the rock-hard soil, every
cat in the neighbourhood started to use it as a lavatory.

They seemed to have a kind of grape-vine that tipped them off about any newly dug ground.

I suppose when you've been brought up to think that every penny has to be spent on food or clothes, and as you can't eat or wear flowers, it becomes ingrained in you that it's a waste of money to buy them. Lovers have been advised to 'Say it with Flowers'. Mine didn't. I was never given flowers by boyfriends. Very few working-class girls ever were. They might buy a quarter-pound of chocolates, which if you went to the pictures you ate as fast as you could, otherwise they'd scoff the lot. Nowadays when I'm asked to open a Bazaar or a Fête, I'm often presented with a bouquet. I appreciate the thought but I take it round to my mother, who does love flowers. Sometimes I think she enjoys collecting the yards of ribbon they're done up with even more than the flowers themselves. Flowers are very nice for people who like them, but I could live without them quite easily.

The Royal Hospital Gardens are ideal for the purpose of the Show. There's a flat bit of ground for the marquee to go, and what a marquee it is. It covers over three and a half acres, and in case like me you can't visualize an acre, that's a lot of ground. In it are all the collections of flowers, fruit and vegetables. Around the marquee and lining the various paths are sort of little shops displaying everything to do with gardens except the plants and flowers: machines and garden tools, insecticides, garden furniture, greenhouses and fertilizers. If you had something of everything shown you'd have to use your house as the garden shed. I had a plan of the marquee and the grounds but I still had great difficulty in locating the various exhibits. I could easily tell where a particular thing was on the plan, what I couldn't work out was where I was in relation to it.

My escort and I made our way into the marquee. The

first thing that struck me was the wonderfully fresh, almost overpowering smell of the flowers – in a way it was claustrophobic. Then I heard a creaking sort of sound: one that was familiar to sailors of old. It was the canvas of the marquee. There was only a light breeze outside but it felt as if it was likely to take off at any moment. I didn't care for it. I'm not a good sailor and I began to get that sinking feeling in my stomach. However, nobody else looked concerned, which was some relief, and after a couple of minutes I got my sea legs.

The first thing I wanted to see was the aviary which had been designed by Lord Snowdon, I suppose because it had got more publicity than anything else in the Show. Other people had the same idea, as there was a crowd there. I didn't think there was anything very spectacular about it. It was done in sections from the centre which meant that it was necessary to walk round it to view all the inmates. If I'd bought one I would have wanted the notice as well which said 'Designed by Lord Snowdon'. It would be one-upmanship. But it's something I've never desired; I don't really like birds, not in confined spaces. I can't stand being in a room where birds are fluttering around. They give me the horrors.

Parrots don't. I like parrots. When I was charring in one place there was a parrot there, a grey one that could talk. It used to come and sit on my finger, then crawl up my arm and on to my shoulder. It was a friendly thing. It never once bit me. And parrots don't flutter around; they're too dignified and have a sort of wise look. I like our wild birds too. I put stuff out for them in the winter; I just want to feel they're around. It's a collective thing; I couldn't feel anything personally for a particular bird.

I'd satisfied my curiosity over Lord Snowdon's aviary, and now turned my attention to the flowers. I started with the roses. Silhouetted against a particularly brilliant display was Harry Wheatcroft, looking as colourful as his collection. He was signing catalogues which were selling like hot cakes. I couldn't help wondering if the crowd around him were as interested in the roses as collecting the autograph of a celebrity. I like Harry Wheatcroft. I admire people who come from nothing, and through hard work and native intelligence reach the top without ever forgetting or letting other people forget their origins. Some call it inverted snobbery. I call it honesty. He looks for all the world like a costermonger with his wild hair, bushy beard and rubicund face.

Some of his roses have classy names, like 'Queen Elizabeth' and 'Duke of Windsor', but Harry sells them all with a Nottingham accent. It's a funny thing about the names, though; the enormous and brilliant rhododendrons were called names like 'Elsie', 'Edith' or 'Miss Crisp' – which just shows one doesn't need a title to be likened to a flower.

There's no question but that you can have too much of a good thing. I did with roses. To relieve the monotony of beauty I looked around at the spectators – mostly ladies, I suppose because it was a weekday. Some of their fashions outdid the exhibits. In fact I almost mistook an elderly female for one. She wore so many colours. Talk about 'On with the motley'. It's strange that when flowers are massed together the colours don't seem to clash but make one harmonious whole; yet a woman in several colours looks an absolute mishmash. I suppose it's because flowers are divine and we are not.

One thing I did notice was an absence of hats. This wasn't surprising since the competition at head level was too great. One woman did enter the lists in a show hat decorated with yellow daisies (or were they sunflowers?); anyway she stuck out like a very sore thumb. I came across her and her hat several times during my perambulations. Was it my imagination, or did that hat get more and more floral every time I saw it? Well, it would be one way of shoplifting.

Many of the spectators were keen gardeners, and it seems that gardening keeps you fit – fighting fit. I have never had to struggle so hard for position or had so many sharp elbows dug into me. These people were gluttons for free information and advice. One formidable enthusiast even had a plan of her garden drawn on a large card and stopped from time to time to get the man in charge of his exhibits to show her where a particular flower should go. I followed her in curiosity for a bit. She came to some azaleas and after a chat handed up her card to have it marked. When she got it back she said, 'Oh, you've put it in my lilies.' It sounded for all the world as if he'd committed some sort of indecent floral assault.

I'd never realized that there were such dedicated gardeners. I saw one walking around sort of measuring out, glancing at the exhibits and then pointing her fingers into the ground, I suppose where she thought she would plant them, and muttering what seemed to me strange incantations as though she was performing some ancient fertility rite.

My escort crossed himself and we moved on.

The orchids' section attracted a lot of attention, particularly from the younger set. I was told that orchids are much hardier than they look, but then so are the debs. Orchids on their own didn't mean a lot to me, but I could imagine some of the blooms made into the most beautiful sprays or even bouquets, though imagination boggles at what that would cost! From the number of exhibitors you'd think that orchids were a commonplace plant but I've never seen any in the gardens and greenhouses I've been in. One exhibitor was very pleased to talk about them. He said they were *Monocotyledons*, all

Greek to me which wasn't surprising because when I asked the derivation of the name 'orchid', he coloured up a bit, looked around at the young faces and whispered in my ear, 'It's the Greek for testicle.' I'm afraid I burst out laughing and it was the kind of laugh that would leave no doubt in the minds of those listening that I'd heard something rude. Mind you, testicles they may be, but they're too rare and expensive to be allowed to propagate on their own. The gardener does it for them.

If I'd ever thought about becoming a gardener, that Show convinced me that it wasn't on. It seemed to me that as well as a grower of flowers, I'd need to be a scientist, pest controller, and a propagation and fertilization expert. A lifetime study. But, judging from the enthusiasts around me, there are a lot of people with this expertise, and the amount of money that was being spent on it amazed me. People who from their clothes looked as though they lived in 'Poverty Street' were blithely ordering roses and rhododendrons by the dozen. One man who looked like a tramp was talking to another 'gentleman of the road' about his head gardener.

'Splendid fellow, Harry, been with me thirty years, knows just how I like everything – worth his weight in gold.'

I couldn't believe my ears. I felt like saying you should see my head gardener, my husband Albert, he's also head painter, decorator, and washer-upper, I've got him for life and he doesn't cost me a penny – and he's worth *more* than his weight in gold.

I was tired of flowers by now – so we made for the vegetables. Here was beauty and utility. The National Farmers' Union exhibition was out of this world. The smoothest, reddest tomatoes, all exactly the same size, the symmetrical onions and leeks, the well-hearted cabbages and lettuce, the greenness of the watercress – it was as though the pictures on the seed packet had come to life.

Wandering around this display was like being Alice in Wonderland, with everything a bit unbelievable. Never in any greengrocer's have I seen goods even remotely resembling this marvellous display. I said as much to one of the attendants. He stuck his chest out a bit with pride and said, 'We grow everything like that and that's how we sell them. It's what happens to them afterwards that you want to complain about. The fruit and the vegetables get rough handling. The middleman doesn't care and the retailer has no idea of display.' He showed a feeling of success in craftsmanship, a pleasure in having accomplished something by planting, tending and cultivating that isn't passed on to those who handle the finished product.

As I looked at this magnificent and beautiful array, I wondered why we needed or wanted to join the Common Market. Here was this wonderful British food which would sell at British prices. Europe should join us, not us them. Our farmers are not appreciated nearly as much as they should be. They deserve a greater recognition. Theirs is hard work and long hours. I know people say they've never seen a poor farmer, but if people with the 'eight to five' or the 'nine to six' mentality had to work the hours that a farmer does there'd be a general strike. As for the conditions they work in ... well!

I spend a bit of time in pubs, and publicans are always telling me how hard they work, but theirs is a social life lived in warmth and jollity. You can't have a social life with pigs and cows for company or when you're ploughing fields, can you?

By now, after three hours sort of window-shopping, my enthusiasm was beginning to wane. I wasn't alone in this. Some of the conversations around were getting distinctly acrimonious. As they grew accustomed to the exhibits, wives were comparing them with their husbands' efforts at home. 'Why can't you do this?' 'Why can't you do that?' And I thought how understandable it was that the replies were mostly caustic, for such exhibits aren't grown as a hobby at weekends. Familiarity had bred contempt; what had started off as 'unbelievable', 'marvellous', 'glorious' was now given a cursory 'Yes, quite nice', or 'Quite pretty' or 'It's all right', followed by 'If I don't take the weight off my feet soon I'll pass out' or 'Where's the refreshment tent?'

I echoed this last conversational snatch and my escort and I took a breather over a cup of tea, quickly served, incidentally, and well worth drinking. Unfortunately, seats were as rare as orchids so we had to continue to stand. I wasn't sorry for this, as I find that once I sit down after a lot of walking I seldom want to get up again.

I looked through the guide and realized that there was much we hadn't seen, and, from the condition of my feet, we were not going to see it. I could understand that the enthusiastic would spend a few hours there on every day of the Show. I fancied a look at the strawberries – I shouldn't have. Like all the others around I stood there and drooled. Great succulent berries budding from every stem. Could they really have been grown like that all ripe for plucking, or had they been fixed on by hand? I couldn't get near enough to find out. From a distance they reminded me of the wax fruit under a glass case that my grandmother always kept in that 'holy of holies', the front parlour. It stood next to the one-eyed stuffed owl, who stared at me as if he'd uncovered all my trespasses. I thought the waxed fruit was real and had been preserved in some kind of embalming fluid, like that used on Egyptian mummies. There were also several pin-cushions made to look like tomatoes. When my grandmother died, we threw them all away. They'd be collectors' pieces now – another fortune in the dustbin. Those strawberries did for me. I'd had a surfeit of perfection, so we joined the ranks of those who were leaving.

The journey to the gate made an interesting and amusing picture. It reminded me of an advertisement for somebody's medicated bath salts which shows a saggy old Mary going into the bathroom, and an upright, bright Mary leaving it. Only with me it was the reverse. I'd walked in like those latecomers who were passing us light of heart and step, and I was going out limp of foot and glazed of eye. Mentally, I'd been grossly overfed, although I'd enjoyed myself. It had been an experience and would be useful as a conversational gambit, but I tried to imagine my feelings if I'd been a keen gardener. Far from encouraging me, which I imagine is the intention of the Show, I think I would have gone back home, dug up any garden I had and planted grass seed. But perhaps the striving is all. And then I remembered the many exhibits that showed how to turn your lawn into a beautiful weed-free green carpet – the envy of your neighbours. It seems to me that in the horticultural world you can never win.

THE YEOMEN OF THE GUARD

The Queen's Bodyguard of the Yeomen of the Guard, Inspection by Her Majesty the Queen at Buckingham Palace this Wednesday, June 24th, 1970

WHEN I received an invitation card with Buckingham Palace written across the top of it, I must admit that besides the excitement of it I felt a kind of pride tinged with vanity, to think that I personally was asked to view the Queen inspecting her Yeomen. My spirits fell slightly when I saw that the card said 'Admit Bearer'; it didn't invite me by name; and my enthusiasm was even further dampened when I read that in the event of wet weather the inspection would take place privately. It was raining cats and dogs at the time and looked as if it was likely to continue doing so for the rest of the month.

However, I let my imagination wander and I could picture myself arriving at Buckingham Palace, being shown to my seat by a flunkey, and bowing slightly to acknowledge his attention – my usual delusions of grandeur, in fact. In the event, it was not like that at all. I had to go to a side entrance in Buckingham Palace Road. I couldn't have missed it because there was a long queue of people, all clutching tickets like mine, who, judging by their windswept appearance, had been waiting there some time. I tagged on at the end of the line and got my buffeting from the elements so that when the doors were opened much of the sense of the dignity of the occasion had gone along with my original band-box appearance. As we got into the Palace grounds, the rest went; as, led by the more knowing ones, everybody broke into a sort of gallop towards the terrace to get a front-row seat. I, naïve in these matters, thought that, as the ticket was numbered, it would correspond with a seat. It was supposed to, but try convincing a determined woman who'd just done a hundred yards in ten seconds flat that she's sitting in the wrong seat! As a rule I've always been able to hold my own in this kind of scrummage; I've had plenty of practice at the sales and my elbows are the terror of Brighton and Hove but I prefer the close game, and here I was outclassed. I had to content myself with a seat in the third row.

As I've said, I had imagined our reception would be vastly different. All right, when you stand waiting in the street to catch a glimpse of Royalty, you don't expect any attention. But, with a ticket, you feel someone and it's a bit of a shock to find you're not. It's all vanity, I suppose.

Another thing that made our entrance so incongruous was that most of the ladies, and the majority attending were ladies, were dressed as though they were going to Ascot: in flimsy summer frocks and large wide-brimmed hats. I thought I'd got myself up well for the occasion, but I hadn't gone to town as most of the others had. Many of them appeared to know each other and it seemed to me they must go regularly to these events. They spoke well too, that is if you like cultured accents, and looking at them I could tell that they were the kind unused to queueing at the theatre or cinema. But for this particular occasion they were prepared to put themselves on a par with people like me, to take their places in the queue, and they didn't seem to resent it. They stood there nattering away to each other despite the perishing cold – the fire of patriotism must have warmed them from within.

I could understand their enthusiasm. They were going to get not just a fleeting glimpse of the Queen, which is all most people ever have, but a ringside seat and time to study her movements and expressions. They were going to experience something that the common ruck of people can't. Today they were special, and the event would be something exciting for them to talk about.

As I surveyed the scene from my seat, I saw the class system personified. On the terrace the chairs were set out in three groups: in the centre group they were gold-painted, with red damask seats. These were for the people waiting inside the Palace, higher up the social ladder than me and my companions; VIPs and friends of the Queen.

On either side of these red damask chairs were green wooden ones with upholstered seats. These were occupied by people who'd come in through the main Palace entrance, but were not grand enough to go into the Palace itself – sort of friends of friends of the Queen, I thought. Then there was us on wooden slatted seats. As I surveyed us, I hastily moved to the front edge of my seat because, by the very nature of the chair's construction, if you sat back your rear stuck out between the two side-pieces. Most undignified it was. Just like those twin-tyres at the back of a lorry!

When I was sure I was properly adjusted, I started to think about this seat distinction. Either everybody should have a gold-painted chair with a red damask seat or everybody should sit on a hard wooden chair. I expect some people to have more comfort than others if they're paying for it, but I didn't expect to see such an example of class distinction at Buckingham Palace. I'm not one of those people who say that everyone should be the same –

of course we shouldn't. Obviously the more money you've got the more comfortable your life is going to be, whether you've acquired your money by hard work or whether you've inherited it, it makes no difference. But when you're invited to see the Queen inspecting her Yeomen of the Guard, where money doesn't count, why should the sheep be separated from the goats?

We sat there about twenty minutes before anything happened. I'd just started humming 'Where are the Yeomen, the Yeomen of England?' when they came into the ground, and a fine sight they were, marching with perfect precision, flanked by the band of the Irish Guards.

These Yeomen were formed by Henry VII in 1485, have maintained an unbroken service ever since, and for the first three hundred years they alone were responsible for the safety of the sovereign. This and the sight of them marching towards us made me feel proud of my country, however corny that may sound, or however much of a cliché. Here was a living tradition and a good one – not something that had become a tradition because it benefited a certain class of people.

When I've seen Yeomen on the stage or at a fancy-dress dance the costume has always seemed incongruous if not laughable. But, worn by these men and in this setting, it looked splendid and right. They were not young men yet they stood upright and alert. You felt each man was an individual despite his uniform. The whole assembly had more reality, more character, than the usual parade of soldiers.

The Yeomen are chosen from all three Services, and are men who've merited the honour, not necessarily through acts of bravery but because of the good service they have given to their country. They are the cream and they behaved as the cream should. I had the opportunity of meeting some of them afterwards, and they made me feel they were proud to be Yeomen, proud to belong to the Queen, and proud that they'd been selected. It was an honour they'd earned through their attitude to their work, yet one that they had not consciously worked for.

While we were waiting for the Royalty and nobility and the red-damask-seated spectators to appear, I looked round, thinking, I must make the most of it; I may never get in here again, especially after the book comes out. There wasn't much to see, some large stone Grecian urns on the balustrade with one or two writhing snakes round them; I don't think they were real Grecian urns, they were just made out of cement. The Palace grounds are now overlooked by tall blocks of flats, offices and hotels. It can't be pleasant for the Queen to feel that even when taking her ease in her garden she may be being stared at through binoculars or photographed by a long-range camera. Whoever you are, whether your garden is measured in feet or acres, you like to feel that you have some privacy in a very public world. When I sit in my back yard in a bathing costume, nobody can see me, not that they're missing all that much, aesthetically at any rate. But that can't be said for the grounds at the Palace, and the Queen wouldn't want to sunbathe under a tree. I don't blame her for going away to Sandringham or Windsor pretty frequently. There she gets the privacy for which she must long. It's one thing having people stare at you when you know they're there, quite another when you feel them watching yet aren't able to see them. Lack of privacy was one of the reasons I didn't like living on a council estate. Inside the houses the walls are so thin that you only have to be there a week and you know your next-door neighbours intimately, even though you may never have spoken to them. Outside in the garden, and most councils give you a nice bit of garden, all you've got is a wire fence between you and the next one. There's no privacy at all. Give me my back yard every time. Heaven knows I'm a gregarious person. I like people. But I think we all like them more if we can get away from them from time to time. It's getting harder to do that. If you're poor, you're squashed and jostled in buses, supermarkets and on crowded pavements. If you're well-to-do then you're busy with your social life, your entertaining, and either making telephone calls or answering them.

If there'd ever been any doubt in my mind as to the origin of the expression 'Getting the red-carpet treatment', it would have been dispelled by what I saw on this morning. There, leading from a Palace room behind us, stretching right across the garden to the gold-painted damask-seated chairs, lay this red-tufted prize Axminster. Why a carpet and why is it always red? The servants and the gardeners keep the place clean and, after all, a terrace is a terrace, and flagstones can't be too hard on the feet.

Someone once suggested to me that the custom descends from Sir Walter Raleigh, Queen Elizabeth, the puddle and the cloak. I doubt it, though. I've always rather cared for that story or legend. That to my mind was chivalry, and I like chivalry. Possibly because I don't see a lot of it.

But this red-carpet treatment is not chivalry, it's ostentation. It's advertising to all and sundry that someone special is coming. Don't tell me that the Queen really enjoys treading on carpet, or that she does it all the time. No, it's not for her benefit. It's become a sort of 'keeping-up-with-the-Joneses' thing amongst the people who entertain her.

While I was mentally griping away about this carpet, the doors of the Palace room opened and out came the red-damask chair customers. They trooped across the carpet and sat in their places. Then, to my complete astonishment, a Palace servant appeared with a broom and brushed every inch of the carpet across the terrace and down the steps to where the Queen was to be. The stupidity of it! In the first place the carpet wasn't dirty, and in the second even if there had been a speck or two of dirt the Queen wouldn't have minded – after all, she was only going to walk on it, not roll on it. If I'd been one of the red-damask chair spectators, I'd have taken umbrage. It made it look as if they'd got dirty feet or trodden in something. I thought it a lot of downright poppycock. A woman sitting next to me said, 'Wouldn't it be funny now if a bird flew over and dropped something in the middle of the carpet?' 'You obviously don't know the birds around here,' I said. 'They're all so well trained that when they want to do their business they fly over Lord Nelson.'

Eventually her Majesty appeared, accompanied by a symphony of 'oohs' and 'aahs' from those around me. 'Isn't she beautiful!' I heard some murmuring. Now I think it's absurd to exaggerate and to try to make the Queen out as some sort of film star. She's a nice, pleasant-looking woman, the sort of person I'd like to have for a neighbour, that's what I feel about her. That's the way I think most people feel about her. If she looked like a film star she might start behaving like one, and that would never do. 'Oh, I've never seen the Queen in that colour before,' said a woman near me, as though she had an intimate knowledge of the Queen's wardrobe. Another, wearing a hat of red, white and blue muslin petals, wept with emotion. I reckoned that both things were carrying patriotism too far.

There's a school of thought that says the Queen's clothes are frumpish. I don't go along with this. Being a Queen, she can't wear outlandish clothes; nor should she be a fashion-plate, it doesn't go with being a Queen. She's got to give the impression of someone who's eminently sensible, for although she doesn't run the country she is consulted about things and her every word is respected and repeated, at any rate by most people. So, even though she may not write the words herself she's got to sound and look as though she believes them, and she wouldn't do this in outlandish garments with tatty hair, beads, chains and knee-high boots.

I was always taught at school to be careful with the word 'nice', that it was grossly misused, but I think it applies to our Queen.

The inspection didn't take long, but was well worth the waiting for. I particularly noticed the fearsome-looking weapons these Yeomen carry, their pikes and halberds. It was interesting to see that they have the letters E R engraved on them. It's good to know that you don't just get stabbed *in* the Queen's name but *with* the Queen's name!

The Queen inspected the Yeomen in the company of what I assumed to be their Commanding Officer. She chatted to almost every one of them and although naturally I couldn't hear everything that was said I got the impression that there was nothing condescending in her attitude towards them. I think I could tell this from the expression on the men's faces; and that she was as interested in them as they were in her. It made it a personal thing, and it was fascinating to observe this kind of relationship between the Queen and her Bodyguard.

When the ceremony was over, the red damask seats filed back into the Palace again in front of the Queen. Was the servant going to appear again to sweep the carpet, I wondered? He didn't. I supppose because their feet had not been sullied by contact with the ground. This move was the signal for a stampede from my part of the audience as they rushed to form two ranks through which the Queen would have to pass, all anxious for a glance from those Royal eyes or a smile from the Royal lips. I stayed to watch from my seat. Not because I disapproved of what my fellow companions were doing – after all, the motives that prompted them were harmless enough – but because I preferred to keep the image of a natural Queen talking naturally to her Yeomen; men who were as near and dear to her as she was to them.

ETON

v

HARROW

IT seems that Sport has become the way of life and that the calendar is divided into the seasons of Horse Racing, Rowing, Cricket, Golf, Tennis and Football. When I was young, people played for fun and for exercise and watched for enjoyment. Sport was considered to promote friendship. It was something that destroyed the boundaries of nations, class and creed. Today it builds them.

Perhaps it could be described as a war substitute. If so that's no bad thing, but let us recognize it for what it really is and not go on deceiving ourselves.

Some of the sport which is part of the London Season still retains much of its old character. In many cases for some people it's only used as an excuse for a social occasion. That's how I looked at it.

I was disappointed to find that the first time I was to attend an Eton and Harrow cricket match, it was held at Harrow, not at Lords as it used to be. I've never been to Lords but the name sounds as though it really is something. In politics we have the House of Commons and the House of Lords, and not only does the House of Lords sound finer but if you read the speeches that are made there, the standard of thinking and debate is not only better but more rational. I suppose this is because they're not bogged down by the Party line; they just say what they think. After all, when you are a Lord you don't have to worry about your image – it's there with you all the time. You can afford to tell the truth.

Cricket and Lords reminds me of an incident in one of my jobs as a kitchenmaid. The family had been to the Eton and Harrow match that day. The nephew was at Harrow, and they'd brought back a large party for dinner. This, in itself, was enough to put the cook into a bad temper, but, to add fuel to her fire, Matthew the footman had been rude to her; he'd cast doubts on the authenticity of some of her stories of the aristocratic people she'd worked for. She then cast doubts on his ancestry, and a first-class row ensued.

This footman was very handsome and really an absolute charmer, but his charm didn't extend to the kitchen, probably because the cook was fat and fifty-ish. I, like any kitchenmaid, was less than the dust. Mr Barnes, the butler, also liked Matthew, so the cook's comments about him fell on deaf ears.

After dinner was over above stairs, and the servants were having stew for their meal, Matthew said, 'Did you hear what the Governor said about cricket? That it's a game for gentlemen and only gentlemen play it.'

Up spoke the cook: 'In that case it's certain none of you would know anything about it, let alone play it.'

Up got the butler: 'It's evident that you do,' he said, picking up one of the dumplings. 'This bloody thing would pass for a cricket ball on any ground. Here! Catch!' and he slung it at her.

Talk about a wet wicket! It caught her in the middle of her chest and made a splodgy sort of sound. 'Out,' shouted Matthew, and put his finger up. Out went the cook screaming blue murder. She repaired the damage, then went upstairs and gave in her notice. The case went for arbitration next day – there were apologies all round, tears from the cook and much inward laughter from me. Harmony reigned for a week or two. Eventually, though, Matthew got the sack. Apparently there was some liaison between him and a guest of the house, a very wealthy widow, who used to stay from time to time. They got married. We didn't see either of them again. Quite a fairy tale it was, except that she was thirty years older than him! A sort of fairy godmother.

One of the main snags of holding the Eton and Harrow match at Harrow is the drive out there from London. Perhaps my escort and I made a mistake in taking the Harrow road, but it sounded the obvious one. We went through grey, dingy places like Willesden, Harlesden and Kensal Rise, a depressing experience. I lived in those parts before the war so I know something about them. When people say what an exciting place London is to live in, they ought to try living in a tenement home in a dreary suburb. It's no more like Chelsea or Kensington than Wigan Pier.

Eventually we got to the Green Belt country and Harrow-on-the-Hill. Still a village, gracious and unspoilt except by the constant traffic. We had drinks and lunch at the King's Head which I imagine must be the school pub where parents take their sons for a meal on visiting days. There were a number of parents, and old boys of both schools, and the bar chat was all cricket. The usual name-dropping was going on. It seems to me that the past masters of cricket are remembered far more than in any other sport. Men like W. G. Grace, C. B. Fry, Bradman and Hobbs are still compared with present-day cricketers. This doesn't seem to apply to football – anyway, the sort that's played with a round ball. Perhaps because that game has altered so much so quickly. Just as rabbits and hares used to be the working man's shooting, and whippets and greyhounds their hunting, so soccer was their sport, to be played and watched under tough and arduous conditions.

There was no real money in football for the players

and it cost little for the spectators. Today it's like a ballet, with players dancing nimbly round an arena. When two in different colours meet with the ball, one of them falls down like some human sacrifice and writhes on the ground, waiting for an elderly dancer to blow his whistle. Eventually, and sooner rather than later if the whistle doesn't blow, the dying figure springs to his feet and rushes around with his previous gay abandon. If by any chance the ball goes into one of the nets at each end of the arena, this is the signal for a sex orgy; the performers hug and jump at each other until the whistle goes and the ballet begins once again. This is all performed to the accompaniment of cheers, boos, handclaps and occasional missiles from the audience who sit around in comfort in rows of seats that reach up to the sky.

Football is also interesting sociologically since it is the only remaining example in Britain of the slave trade. Players are openly bought and sold in the market place and although their owners give them a lot of spending money, it bears no relation to the amounts that change hands. After such a transaction, the player, his wife and children are carted off to wherever the buyer lives and there they remain until another similar financial transaction is set up.

But, getting back to my argument that cricket is still played in the same way, it is, except there are no longer any gentlemen, they're all players. I wonder why they abolished gentlemen and not players! They still wear the same gear; the grounds are very much as they were; and both teams now come out of the same gate. The only way I think it's changed is that the players today are so much younger. I was told by my escort that that is because I'm so much older, but I don't think it's just that or the fact that in the old days they used to wear beards. I think men grew old quicker when I was young.

After lunch, also taken to the accompaniment of cricket talk, we walked down to the ground. I must say I found the scene disappointing. All right, the field was next to the imposing school buildings but it had the appearance of a back yard. I'd expected idyllic surroundings – tranquillity and peace with only the sound of leather ball on willow bat disturbing the quiet of the afternoon. A place where the loveliness of the surroundings would be matched by the 'beauty of youth in all its magnificence'. Instead I found a sort of glorified public recreation ground with iron railings at the bottom, alongside of which the traffic roared past; the wind blew dust into my face; and a scant collection of spectators all grouped around a marquee near the pavilion were looking thoroughly cold and miserable. I couldn't blame them. I sat on a bench to get into the spirit of the game. I tried to put myself inside the hearts of those boys who were out there defending the honour of their school. I recalled all the books I'd read, not only in my youth but later in life, like *Tom Brown's Schooldays, This England,* and that poem – what is it? '...last man in and one run to win.' I remembered all the thrills I'd got from reading, so, how much greater, I thought, would it all be in reality. It wasn't. Over after over was bowled with the occasional run being scored. The players seemed as unconcerned about the event as the schoolboy spectators, most of whom stood in groups away from the field of play both mentally and physically. Perhaps it was the weather. Perhaps cricket's main ingredient is sunshine. I've found it a lovely game to watch on a hot summer's day; I've sat in the Sussex ground at Hove and had most restful times daydreaming. One eye on the game, one eye shut, my mind in limbo. If you doze off for half an hour, you can be sure you haven't missed anything.

Cricket's been labelled as a 'typical British sport'. It

isn't. It's quite unique. Typical British sports are both foul and farcical, like fox-hunting. Doing it is foul, then justifying it by saying the fox likes it is farcical. To pretend that a fox enjoys careering over the countryside chased by a pack of hounds knowing that if it's caught it's going to be torn to pieces. Balderdash!

Stag-hunting is plain diabolic. Shooting is easier to justify because there is something to eat at the end of it, though too often pheasant and partridge shoots are an excuse for a massacre.

The 'noble art' of boxing is another ludicrous, twisted expression. What's noble about going into an arena to watch two men try to bash the living daylights out of each other, and booing them if they don't? And don't tell me that the boxers enjoy it. If they did, why do they have to be paid so much money to go into the ring?

People talk about violence on television, and set up committees to report about it. They ought to start on the sporting scene. That would keep them busy for a very long time. As for the idea that sport promotes friendship between countries, recent events have shown that that's one for the archives.

You see what I mean about my mind being in limbo during a cricket match. While I was watching Eton versus Harrow, my thoughts were wandering elsewhere. I even found myself wishing that we could have a spot of violence to warm things up.

I suppose to a lover of cricket it doesn't matter if there isn't a lot of running about, but four runs in half an hour was for me, to say the least, boring.

I decided now to concentrate my attention on the spectators who were mainly grouped around the pavilion and the marquees where tea and drinks were being served. They were a motley lot. I'd expected to see a miniature Ascot with all the men in morning suits carrying gloves and toppers; but most of them wore either light-coloured suits or sports jackets. The mothers of the boys were extremely smart, though it was difficult to define their fashions. It was as though they had been told by their sons to appear well dressed but not 'way out'. Individually they looked delightful but the effect of the whole scene was wishy-washy.

The girls for the most part had done their particular thing – mini, midi and maxi mixed with some decorative trouser-suits. They added brightness and colour but again, fashion-wise, it seems that the 'Seventies' have begun with no clear indication of the direction it is taking. One thing that struck me about the younger set is that dress today is a great leveller. It's impossible to tell a deb from a shopgirl.

I suppose I shouldn't be proud of eavesdropping but with the upper crust it's often difficult not to. They tend to talk in conversation as if they are addressing a public meeting. I'd heard that both Eton and Harrow were more like clubs than schools. That you were sent there not because of the kind of education you would receive but for the boys you'd meet and get to know; so that when you left school, through your friends and their parents you'd have the kind of contacts that would help you not only to get your first job, but throughout your career.

I wasn't sure whether to believe it or to put it down to sour grapes on the part of those who hadn't been there. Anyway, one particular conversation I couldn't help overhearing went like this:

'Harry, hello – I was hoping I'd bump into you.'

'Hallo, Charles, good to see you. That boy of yours was in amongst the runs today [referring to Charles' son who was playing in the match].'

'Yes, good show, and it was about him I wanted a word. He's dead set on the diplomatic service after Oxford, and we wondered if you could give him a bit of a helping hand.'

'Oh [not enthusiastically]. Has he thought about the Foreign Office?'

'Not keen, it's the diplomatic or nothing with him.'

'I see [stalling]. I still think the FO might be more in his line.'

'Well, what about seeing him and chatting about it? I'm sure then you'll be convinced that he's diplomatic material. Shall we say lunch next week?'

'Well, I'm a bit busy ... [weakening].'

'Let's say next Friday. Things are normally a bit quieter towards the weekend. Savoy Grill, one o'clock all right?'

'All right [surrender] – I'll look forward to it. Can't promise too much, though [keeping a way out if necessary].'

'Not to worry, I know you'll do your best. Look forward to seeing you.'

And Charles rejoins the ladies flushed with victory.

I'd never seen the 'Old Boys' net' at work before and I was fascinated. Don't think I'm knocking it. What parents wouldn't do the same for their sons, given the opportunity? I know that I got all the grants I could for mine. On the other hand, don't let's pretend that this isn't what privileged education is all about.

Later, I chatted to a group of debs, all of whom had brothers at one school or the other. I asked where they were. 'Over with their friends,' they replied.

'But don't you want to be with them?' I inquired, and got the Pygmalion reply: 'Then why do you come? Are you fond of cricket?'

'You're too priceless,' one said. 'I wouldn't watch this boring game if you paid me in the ordinary course of events.'

'Why do you do it now, then?'

'Well, we absolutely have to – it's the Season and we promised our parents that we'd go through with it.'

I'm afraid my escort and I didn't wait for the end of the match. As it got colder and windier, the game got less and less interesting and I found myself agreeing with the debs.

The next day I read an account of 'this exciting match' in *The Times* – which shows you mustn't believe all you read in the newspapers.

HENLEY REGATTA

BEFORE I went to Henley my experience of regattas had been limited to those of my home town, Brighton. The boats they used had sails on them and I believe the course was marked with buoys. But sitting on the pebbles on the beach when the wind is blowing and it's pouring with rain, makes it difficult enough to see the yachts let alone the buoys. Also I had no idea what they were trying to do. At one moment they seemed to be chasing along and then some bloke would shout, round would go the mast and over would go the boat. That last bit used to delight me, and it made the people laugh too.

There were a few who seemed to be watching in solemnity. Presumably they knew what was going on but I hadn't the courage to ask them. You may wonder why I went, but it's like anything else that happens locally, isn't it – you can't imagine it will be as bad as last year. And if you do live by the sea it makes a change to look at it occasionally. There was always the excitement in the evenings too, with the Battle of Flowers, especially when after a while they ran out of flowers and it changed to a battle of lard-bladders filled with water.

When I was very young, we had a game which I used to like playing. Now I'm ashamed and appalled at myself, and I offer no justification for it. At the Regatta, the toffs – the well-to-do, or so they seemed by our standards – used to sit in deckchairs and whenever anything interesting was going on they'd stand up to watch; then we'd crawl up behind and adjust the wood piece so that when they sat down they collapsed on the beach. I know it's not funny now, but we used to scream with mirth.

When I was contemplating going to Henley I didn't imagine it was going to be like Brighton Regatta. I associated it with romance: willow trees, the lapping of the waters by the riverbank, straw boaters with their gay bands, punts, white flannels, long dresses and wide-brimmed hats, romantic love, guitars and all that lark. A bit like I imagined Venice – although somebody once told me that it's a revolting place; smelly canals filled with dead cats and overhung with mosquitoes, and as for the gondoliers serenading you, all they do is look daggers in case you don't pay them enough. Preconceived ideas are dangerous things.

By now I'd realized from the events that I'd been to that the spectators are divided into sheep and goats. The experts and the uninformed. To me at Henley it was super sheep and sheep, because a babe in arms can tell which boats win and how they win. There's the water; there are the boats and oars; and that's it. Those who pull hardest and row fastest win and no bones about it. The chaps who have won sit upright in their boat and those who've lost try to see if they can put their heads between their legs. They can't get out and have a punch-up even if they feel like it, so when they've turned the boat upside down to make sure that nothing has been left inside, they go and drink together. All very nice and uncomplicated.

I believe that on some occasions the crew do throw the cox, who's really the sort of jockey of the boat and is about the same build, into the river. I inquired why this was but nobody seemed to know, so I assume it's because he shouts at them while they are rowing and as they haven't the breath to answer him back they give vent to their feelings later. The whole sport is remarkably simple, remarkably British and therefore remarkably civilized.

Whoever organizes Henley does a fine job. The setting is superb. It's a wonderful stretch of river with a beauty and an atmosphere which is hard to define but which is both preserved and exploited by the organizers.

The super sheep are easy to distinguish. They go around in their old school caps which are far too small for them. They talk louder than other people and seem to know everyone's christian name. If they dressed and behaved like this anywhere else, a van would turn up and whip them off to the nearest asylum; but, apparently, it's all part of the Henley scene. I was charmed and delighted to find that nobody showed any emotion. The races just seemed to be part of a ritual. My escort and I sat by the riverbank on deckchairs in an enclosure near the finishing-post. There was some bellowing towards the end if the crews were fairly near each other, but most of the races seemed to be decided out of our sight in the first half-minute. However, the sun was shining and I felt that this was how life should be but so seldom is.

Another bit of ritual observed by those sitting by the riverbank is that shortly after the first boat has passed, you lift your legs into the air. Then with a swoosh the wash sweeps along the bank. It looks for all the world as if it's going to splash over the bank but it doesn't, so down go your legs ... to be brought up again shortly when the second crew passes. Everyone does this during each race, even though they know they won't get wet; as I've said, it's part of the ritual. Talk about 'Knees up Mother Brown'!

I particularly liked watching the punts on the river. It's not a form of locomotion I've seen much of but the chaps manipulating the poles look graceful and unhurried, and for the passengers it appears to be the most comfortable ride imaginable. I can understand why they were commonplace in the old romantic novels. Nowadays in books all the petting and such like is performed in cars which I reckon is doing it the hard way.

Looking at those punts made me think of what I'd missed out on in my youth. I suppose I'd thought of them more as comic things because of the antics in that book, *Three Men in a Boat*. Mind you, some of the characters on the river were dressed in just such an outlandish way, but I reckon that was the only comparison that could be drawn between them. I half hoped to see the pole caught on the river-bed and the punter clinging to it while the punt moved away, but of course it didn't happen.

One criticism I have about the arrangements at Henley is that either the amplifying equipment is archaic or the men doing the speaking don't know how to use it. Some of the voices too were so la-di-dah as to be incomprehensible. We go to such extremes in this country. Either you get what we did at Henley, or else if you're catching a train you get some character announcing what might well be 'All stations to Delhi, calling at Madras, Bayalore, Calcutta and Tonypandy'.

As incomprehensible to me, even when I could decipher it, was the commentator talking about one crew striking at thirty-four and the other at thirty-six. 'In, out, in, out, in, out,' he called like an undecided bouncer at a pub. I'd never heard of this sort of stroke before. The only kind I knew was the sort a somewhat apoplectic employer of mine was always threatening he would have when I made him laugh. (He was safer laughing than when he got romantic!) However, a group of boys from Bedford School were now standing near us and they explained to me what it meant.

They also got a bit hilarious when I expressed concern for the rowers' trousers. 'Don't they wear out quickly with all that rubbing backwards and forwards?' I asked. Well, as a mother it's a natural reaction. I didn't know that it was the seats that moved, not the behinds. I thought that it was like rugby football where from time to time they have that ceremony with the trousers that get torn. They make a sort of circle round the player and then sling the old shorts over the top of their heads while they study anatomy and fit a new pair. It's always good for a laugh, and heaven knows, with sport today, any form of humour comes as a relief.

In one sort of international race, an English club rowed against a Dutch one. This was an exciting event because in a close finish the English boat was beaten by only three-quarters of a length. I was fascinated to hear the English sporting defence mechanism going into action: 'They went down fighting,' said one man proudly. 'Another hundred yards and they'd have won,' said another. 'If so and so had been in the boat they'd have walked it,' volunteered a third. 'How can they expect to beat Gold Medallists, anyway?'

Next day I read in the newspaper that for once we could praise a British defeat. That one amused me. Nine times out of ten, in international sporting events, you hear and read the same thing. The headlines don't mention the winner, and the article is mostly about why we could or should have won. The writer then castigates some unfortunate person who he knows can't answer back and ends by saying that if his (the writer's) advice had been followed victory would certainly have been ours. We're never allowed to believe that the best side won – which I have always thought to be the point of any game.

I suppose because these two crews were so close together when they passed us, we got a bigger swoosh from the wash. Up went the legs, only a bit higher than usual

– all except those of an American gentleman next door to me. As it happened he didn't get his feet wet. I don't think it was bravado on his part; I think he just wanted an excuse to show off his knowledge of English history, because he started on about his second name being Canute. I don't believe it was, but it might have been; Americans do go in for way-out names like 'King', 'Earl', 'Duke' and 'Tennessee', to name a few that instantly come to mind. Then from Canute and his seaside prank he went on to the other apocryphal snippets of Raleigh and his cloak, Drake and his bowls, Nelson and his blind eye, and Alfred and his cakes. As I pointed out to him, these snippets of information would not further any attempt he was making towards a better understanding of Britain and her people.

The next race was between two school crews. This added a little excitement to the proceedings. Young and old alike seem to attach greater importance to the prowess of these schools than to any of the other events. They were, of course, public schools.

It was all very different from my council school where we had a Sports Day once a year in which we competed against other schools in the district. Most of us not actually taking part couldn't have cared less who won. We were only interested in stuffing ourselves with cakes and swilling them down with lemonade.

This race gave me another opportunity to talk to the boys from Bedford School, who were delightful company. So often, when I come up against people who are better educated than I am, it sets off my inferiority mechanism, and since I rarely meet young people who have had any experience of people like me, I expect to get the kind of treatment I had from my employers' children when I was in service. That, I know, would have made me aggressive, which would put me at a further disadvantage. These boys, though, were easy company without looking as if they were going out of their way to be attentive. Every one behaved naturally; they talked about the intricacies of rowing – which interested me at the time even though I can't remember any of them now.

The American gentleman was also obviously impressed by them, though he found it difficult to understand how a public school was really a private school. Still, it was another British idiosyncracy for him to take back home.

Another peculiar British idiosyncracy is the type and character of the loos provided at sporting events. Those at Henley were no exception. All right, I hadn't expected gold-plated fittings but with the social *élite* there I didn't anticipate hessian cubicles, galvanized buckets, and the modest protection of a flapping canvas at the back. My loo at home can be draughty but I'm certain if I'd taken a newspaper in those at Henley for a quick read I'd have been airborne the moment I opened it. I know that the Henley Regatta is an outdoor event, but this, I thought, was going too far. Still, as the French say, *'Vive le sport'*. As you can imagine, I didn't linger and was back in my deckchair in a matter of seconds.

I've always had a healthy interest in loos. I've been in some quaint ones in my time. Ours is still outside at home. Now we've got a bit of money, people keep trying to persuade me to move it indoors, but I've resisted. It's a kind of hidden snobbery, I suppose. I still enjoy my bath in the kitchen. I sit there with the oven on and the doors open; as I tell Albert, it's better than any centrally heated bathroom.

It was a bit ironic, though, when a short time ago I was after-dinner speaker at some company's dinner at the Hilton Hotel. I had tickets in the tombola competition and was very pleased to get a prize until I was presented with a bathroom set! I'm certain I was the only person there who hadn't got a bathroom and I reckon some of them had two or three!!

In the next race an American boat was competing. My American gentleman, ignoring the behaviour of the British, bellowed out some sort of 'Rah, Rah, Pennsylvania' college cry. Everyone pretended not to notice. I couldn't because he nearly burst my eardrums. He kept it up for the whole race. If encouragement could have done the trick, Pennsylvania would have won; as it was, they were beaten by two and three-quarter lengths. Somebody said this was because they hadn't the right kind of rollocks. That's the worst of being brought up as I was, you can't control the expression on your face and your giggling. It set me off for the rest of the afternoon.

As far as fashions were concerned, it seemed that anything went. Some of the debs wore dresses that their grandmothers could have worn at Henley. Perhaps they *were* the dresses their grandmothers used: tight hobble skirts; flat black hats; black button-up boots and black shawls. I wouldn't have been surprised to see a crinoline. But although the dresses may have been Victorian the girls' false eyelashes, wigs and their kind of language would not have amused her late Majesty.

I enjoyed Henley. It isn't real but it's part of the pageantry of this country. I felt as though I were watching a play while I was there, and I was sorry when the curtain fell. It's not something you want to think about too much. Like the River Thames, just let it take you 'at its own sweet will'.

WIMBLEDON

I'VE always looked on tennis as one of those 'In' games enjoyed by the social *élite*, and as I've never been 'In', I've never played it, watched it, or tried to understand it. I'd heard of Wimbledon first when I was in service and although in recent years it seems to have become an excuse for all kinds of people to sit glued to their television sets during some of the finest days of the year, its early associations are the ones which have stuck with me. A reminder of sharp divisions between 'Them' above and 'Us' below stairs. Then, if the word 'tennis' was mentioned, it meant cutting piles of sandwiches, making dainty cakes, sending the cook into a rage and the parlourmaid into a tizzy. It seemed to me just another reason for a social gathering – 'anyone for tennis?' Nobody, I thought, was really interested in the game itself.

Even when I used to stand around the courts on the front at Hove and watch it, it struck me as a game that only people who had money could play. The very fact that the players were dressed up in white flannels and white dresses meant that it wasn't the kind of game we would ever hope to play; and, of course, as youngsters the scoring – all this 'love-fifteen', 'love-thirty' – used to send us off into peals of laughter. With that way of working out who'd won, it struck us as being a very soppy sort of game and therefore something to sneer at.

This year, Wimbledon for me started when I got into the train at Waterloo Station. The carriage was crowded with tennis enthusiasts who started chatting together in a most fervent way as if discussing matters of supreme importance. Generally, in any conversation, I'm ready to make my contribution but, in this case, knowing so little about the game, I was a bit wary and just listened for a time. One old military-looking buffer was holding forth about the players of yore, the merits of Tilden and Borotra, whose style and power, he maintained, had never been equalled. Taking up the cudgels for the modern school were a young, 'with-it' couple, who compared the old game to vicarage tennis. 'Dog-collared' players like those the old buffer had mentioned, hadn't a place alongside giants like Laver and Rosewall, not to mention the American women.

'What about Mademoiselle Lenglen?' I volunteered. 'What stamina she had. She won five years in a row.' I wasn't quite sure of my facts but I felt someone had to spring to the old man's defence.

The 'with-it' girl hooted with derisive laughter. 'She was about as fast as my old grandmother is at croquet!'

In no time at all, the whole carriage was having a furious debate. I shut up. I'd dropped the only name I knew.

My escort met me at the station and after a short drink we reached the Mecca of the tennis world.

I must say my first impressions of Wimbledon were not very favourable – it seemed to be all concrete and stands, just like a football ground; very much a commercial-looking enterprise, and this couldn't just be because the players had turned professional, because obviously the stands and concrete had been there for years.

I was first taken to watch the Men's Singles on Number One Court. This meant a long climb since our seats were way up aloft. When we got into our places, we seemed perched in mid-air; it was like sitting on Mount Everest and about as hard, as we hadn't taken the opportunity of hiring a couple of cushions. I didn't feel too safe up there, but I consoled myself by thinking that if the stand gave way the people in the rows below me would break my fall.

While we were waiting for the match to begin there was someone calling out, 'This is your last chance to buy an orange juice,' as though if we missed this opportunity the nectar of the Gods would be denied us for ever. Seated as I was, I felt near enough to Heaven and, suffering as I do from vertigo, definitely in need of a brandy. Meanwhile my escort was working overtime explaining to me what all those white lines were for and what such tennis terms as 'love', 'set' and 'deuce' actually meant.

By this time the two players had come on to the court. They were called Carmichael and Gimeno. After knocking the ball backwards and forwards for a bit, they began their match.

I was astonished to see the intensity with which the spectators followed it; as though they were at the Roman sports watching the gladiators. When finally Carmichael lost, I quite expected to see them rise with their thumbs down, and the loser thrown to the lions.

At times the players seemed far from happy. Once, when Carmichael made a bad shot, he hit the offending ball over the stands in temper. If I'd been the umpire I'd have stopped the game and told him I wouldn't begin it again until he'd found the ball and brought it back. Another time when a player made a bosh shot he turned his racquet to his face and started talking to it, taking it to task for what could only have been his mistake. After one game the whole arena muttered that Gimeno had broken service. Apparently this was a good thing: it wasn't in my kitchen days – especially if we were using the Calport.

I was fascinated by the ball-boys, who are recruited from local schools. They don't get paid; it's considered a favour and a matter of prestige. I couldn't see much prestige in dashing about collecting balls, particularly as the players not only didn't thank them when they were given them, they just didn't seem to notice the boys were there. Not a very good example to the young, I should have thought. If they had ball-girls, dressed like drum majorettes, that would liven up the tennis, particularly when they bent over to pick up the balls. Think of the wolf whistles!

That match over, and while waiting for Margaret Court and Rosemary Casals to play on the Centre Court, we strolled around to look at the fashions and to have something to eat and drink. It always amazes me the amount that people seem to put away when they go to a function, especially if it's an outdoor event. It's not just the ordinary people, many of whom take their own food – I saw obviously upper-crust people leaving the food counters with enough on their trays to feed half a dozen. Everywhere I looked, people's jaws were champing up and down in perpetual motion. It reminded me of a time when I visited my sister. She took me out to show me her cabbage patch – not only to show me, but so that I could listen to it. As I stood there I could hear a chugging and grinding sound: it was hundreds of caterpillars chewing away at the cabbage leaves and eventually reducing them to skeletons.

We made our way to the Centre Court and took our places. Studying the programme, I saw something that made me want to rush round to the changing-rooms and recruit for the Women's Liberation Movement: the vast difference between prize money. The winner of the Men's Singles gets £3,000 but the winner of the Women's Singles gets £1,500. Talk about the half-price sex! It's all wrong.

The game is just as strenuous for women and just as entertaining to watch. And just as many people watch the women's games as watch the men's. People complain about racialism in sport, and politics in sport. I felt like writing a placard and sitting down on the Centre Court, to protest about this other injustice.

I found the match between Margaret Court and Rosemary Casals exciting, despite my smouldering feeling of injustice, and it was a much better-mannered affair. By now I had acquired some faint idea of the rudiments of the game so I was able to add my quota to the clapping at every good shot.

The fashions of the players at Wimbledon excite great interest every year. This surprises me because I'd have thought if you're a good player it doesn't matter what you wear. Obviously, you're going to wear something that allows you the greatest freedom of movement, but whether it's a dress by Teddy Tinling or the little woman round the corner, I wouldn't have thought mattered. This year the fashion was pink knickers and pink tops or coloured-bordered dresses. I can't see that any of those things are worth getting excited about or that they reflect in any way on the general trend of fashions. It isn't as if tennis players are things of beauty and a joy for ever. There are one or two quite good-looking ones but, generally speaking, the more the concentration of spectators is focused on their game and not their faces or figures, the better.

The spectators' clothes were a riot and it would have taken an expert to have explained what was in fashion. There were maxis, midis, minis, trouser-suits, tunic-suits – and one woman was wearing such a conglomeration of garments that I thought she had put on her entire wardrobe in case of fire while she was away from home. And there were the inevitable petal hats. Why are they so popular? I know that they're comfortable to wear but there are other kinds of close-fitting hats. Some women can wear a petal hat and look all right, but flowers don't go with some faces – and there were many faces there they didn't go with.

When the match was over we left the Centre Court to look at players on the other courts. On one, the veterans were playing, amongst them such notables as Drobny and Crawford. There weren't many spectators and I wondered if, as they heard the roars from the Centre Court, the players' thoughts went back to the days when they were the heroes sharing the glory of the Finals. Of all the competitors they appeared to be enjoying themselves most and what they lacked in mobility they certainly made up for by the cleverness of their shots. They may have been a bit paunchy round the waist, but it was good to see someone laugh when he made a bosh shot. I suppose they were playing to win, but I felt for the first time that day that I was watching a game; and a game to me means something which is not work, which you do in your leisure time. You could have fooled me as to whether some of those younger competitors were taking pleasure in it – it looked as though it was a matter of life and death for them.

I don't think it's only the money: it's the prestige, because tennis is now an international game and often the players must feel that they are playing for their country as well as for their own, sometimes quite short, futures.

This business of competition seems to have got pretty out of hand and it destroys the fun of the sport. I'm not saying that this is the rule yet at Wimbledon, but the way things are going it may well become it. I'd gone there expecting to watch a game, but my common sense told me it was no longer a game but another job of work, and

71

people do get irritable over their work, irritable and aggressive at times.

I had the opportunity of watching the boy prodigy Stephen Warboys playing. From what I had read about him I expected to see some sort of manufactured article. He's not a boy who's learnt tennis through what I'd describe as the normal channels, first at school, then at a local club and then by professional training. I have read that he has been taught to play by every means available and from early childhood. Money has been no object. So, I was surprised when I saw him to find that he looked charming and unassuming.

He knew people were watching him largely because he had been so publicized, yet he didn't attempt to show off. I wondered whether because of his type of training he would eventually lose the fun and spirit of the game.

I enjoyed my day at Wimbledon, though for me it could never become an annual pilgrimage. It seems as if we are in danger of taking the flavour out of our sport, as we have done with our food. We are becoming over-scientific, dehumanizing it. I would have preferred a local town or village tournament. Nevertheless, it was obvious that the event was hugely enjoyed, judging by the lively and cheerful crowds, some of whom had queued for hours just to stand inside. And I've no quarrels with enjoyment.

THE RACING SCENE

I SUPPOSE it's because racing is called the 'Sport of Kings' that it plays such an important part in the London Season. I don't know when it was that it got this high-sounding title. I can't believe that Queen Victoria was all that keen on it. She seems to have done her best to ostracize anything that added a bit of fun and gaiety to life; and the fact that racing encouraged gambling would certainly not have amused her. I reckon it was Edward VII who gave it the fashion and glamour that it has. Anyway, it has been closely associated with the monarchy as long as I can remember, and while breeding and owning horses is a rich man's hobby, the thrill and excitement of the racing scene and the fun of picking and backing a horse make it a sport for everyman.

Of course some meetings are more fashionable than others. For my London Season I chose Ascot, Epsom and Goodwood; and I did them in what you might call 'style'; that is, I went into the Members' Enclosure on each occasion.

Not that I reckon it matters in the least if you can't afford Members', Tattersall's or the Grandstand. You can get as much pleasure from standing in the cheaper parts of the course. I think it's an absolute waste of money to go in any of these fancy places – after all, I'm not likely to know anyone in the expensive parts, and no one seems anxious to mingle. I don't know enough about horses to be able to judge their finer points by watching them walking around the paddock and it doesn't much matter where you go for a drink, it's slung at you – take it or leave it, but pay through the nose for it.

Our racecourse at Brighton used to be the best day's outing for very little money that one could have. In the old days before they built all the enclosures and stands, anybody could get right up to the finishing-post and have a marvellous view. Mind you, you needed to keep an eye on the bookmakers to see that they didn't scarper or welsh with your money.

One day when I was there with my parents, my father won fifteen shillings on the last race and fifteen shillings was a fortune at that time. He was laughing and throwing his cap in the air, when suddenly he saw his bookie running hell for leather towards the exit with a dozen people tearing after him. Dad joined the queue swearing and cursing in a way I'd never heard him do before. Naturally, the whole family joined in the chase. I'd never run so fast in my life. But just as the first pursuer had almost caught him, the welsher made a flying leap into a moving car and got away. If all the curses that were heaped on him ever took effect he must have had a violent end. Everyone was reckoning how much money they'd lost. No doubt they exaggerated. We'd really only lost two shillings – that was all Dad had put on the horses. But it cost him a lot more in beer money that night to get his temper back. I know the journey home was the worst I'd ever experienced, and my mother didn't help matters when she said that the bookie looked as though he could have done with the money, poor man.

But when I think about that event now it seems all part of the fun of the racing scene, just as later on in life when Albert and I went to Epsom in Derby Week it was the whelks and winkles, the swings and roundabouts, the gipsies, bookies, and tipsters that made our day; while the beer-drinking in the pubs we stopped at and the raucous singing in the coach made our night going back.

Nowadays, of course, at most race-meetings they've tried to stop you looking for free – in fact you almost do feel like a thief if you enjoy a day out without spending anything.

The first meeting was Royal Ascot in June; and of course my immediate thought when I heard I was going there was, What shall I wear? I must have gone through my wardrobe both mentally and physically a dozen times before I decided that I'd got to buy something specially for the occasion. My ideas of Ascot fashions were those that I remembered from the past – things I'd seen in the newspapers and magazines worn by Lady This or the Duchess of That, things from Dior or Hartnell's. I tried on some pretty outlandish and expensive things in our shops in Brighton. Some of them I liked myself in, but I remembered the effect my psychedelic frock had had on my escort at Queen Charlotte's Ball, so I eventually decided on something reasonably discreet. It cost what I consider a fair amount of money so I was looking at it not just as a oncer for Ascot but as something that I could wear on many other occasions. The hat was a problem – hats are always a problem for me as I have a large head. Practically every hat I buy has to be put on a block and stretched to fit me. Judging by what I saw during the Season, hats are a problem for other people too; many of whom make disastrous attempts to find a solution. I tried hard and, since my escort made no comment on my choice, I think I was successful. Anyway, I felt right in it and, as any woman knows, that's the main thing.

The weather on the day we went was perfect and the setting was splendid. I don't think I've ever seen ground looking greener, and in the enclosure it seemed as if so much care and attention had been lavished on the lawns it would be sacrilege to walk on them. They were like green velvet. Gathered on them was the prettiest collection of girls that I'd ever seen. It was as though a flock of brightly coloured birds had landed there, and as they moved around with their escorts, so the colours changed like a revolving rainbow. Many of the frocks were way out, way up and way down, and the hats were like cartwheels so that when the slightest breeze blew up, up went the hands in unison to the back of the heads like a sort of Swedish drill.

The men all wore the same kind of dress: morning coats with grey or coloured waistcoats and top hats. From the back they looked like camouflaged ladybirds or beetles. Very impressive they were but not the least bit comfortable-looking on such a warm day. They were continually mopping their brows with coloured handkerchiefs or fanning themselves with their top hats.

Ascot Week must be paradise for a wealthy young deb, a time when she is encouraged to display all her charms in a setting that lends itself completely to the occasion. Epsom somehow doesn't; even Ladies' Day – the day of the Oaks, the racing classic for fillies – which I went to was just a larger example of the cosmopolitan racing scene. It's too vast, too windy and dusty. All the young girls I saw there looked as though they'd come straight off the King's Road, Chelsea, without changing. A more motley collection of garments I've seldom seen. All shapes, sizes and colours. Perhaps the clothes were rejects from the boutiques. So many debs seem to be running boutiques nowadays, it's like taking in each other's washing. There were a few I saw leaving their private boxes who'd made an effort, but they were soon lost in the crowd. No, Epsom's a meeting for sensible clothes and in particular sensible shoes – the ground's like rock if it's fine or like a skating rink if it's wet.

I think the spectacle of Epsom during Derby Week is the greatest racing scene in this country, and it still keeps the character it had when I was a young woman. There's all the fun of the fair and they even still have those top-less buses right by the rails where you can get a grandstand view.

I always remember one occasion when Albert and I went to the Derby with my sister and brother-in-law. We saw one of these buses stationed, and we wandered over to it thinking that if we paid a bob each we'd get a grandstand view. Standing by the platform was a man wearing an extremely flashy checked suit, a bowler hat and smoking an enormous cigar. 'Up you go, love,' he said to me, and we climbed on to the top. There a very merry party was going on and we were flummoxed when this check-suited character came up with a bottle of champagne and a plate of smoked-salmon sandwiches. 'Good old Ludo,' everyone was shouting. I suppose his name was Ludovic; I can't think what else it could have been. 'Good old Ludo,' we said as we drank and tucked in. Then we realized to our horror that we had gate-crashed a private party. Next, this Ludo came up to us and said, 'You're pals of Jumbo's. He told me about you. Pity he couldn't make it. Still, let's drink to him.' So, fervently hoping he wouldn't ask us too much about Jumbo, and that Jumbo wouldn't make it after all, we raised our glasses to him. We had a marvellous grandstand view and champagne flowed like water.

Goodwood, on the day I went, merited the description 'Glorious' that it's so often given. It is indeed the most glorious country racecourse some half a dozen miles outside Chichester. It stands on high ground, and all around it is the beautiful green of the Sussex countryside. Every time I sing 'Jerusalem' at the Women's Institute meetings I speak at, when it comes to that bit about 'England's green and pleasant land' I think of Goodwood. The Members' Enclosure there was the most pleasant I'd been in and the clothes more fitting to the surroundings. Generally speaking, everyone seemed more mellow and more at ease there. There were a lot of midi dresses being worn by young and old.

Some of the younger ones reminded me of the illustrations in the Kate Greenaway book – that Victorian poetry book for children. My mother had it. It was one of the prizes that she won at school; full of sweetness and light and sentimentality. There were a lot of illustrations in it of young girls wearing muslin dresses with puffed sleeves threaded with ribbon. The sort of thing that would do for a nightie today. They looked virginal in these outfits, as though they were innocents abroad. But as I listened to them talking I realized that any resemblance to Kate Greenaway's heroines was entirely visual; some of the language would have done credit to a bargee.

One thing that struck me at all three meetings is what a small part the actual racing plays in the whole proceedings. There are usually six races which, on average, take about two and a half minutes each, so that in fact you spend a day out for a quarter of an hour's racing, and for at least half that time the horses and their riders are out of sight.

All right, there's a commentary going on, but that doesn't mean much since the horses they talk about at the beginning never finish in the first three. I know. Those I back always get mentioned three or four times in the first few hundred yards, after which they're never heard of again. Why they allow horses with so little stamina in a race I don't know.

It was interesting that both at Epsom and Ascot a lot of people watched the racing on television from the bars. I reckon they saw more that way than pinned against the rails; and with a glass in their hands to celebrate if they won and as consolation if they lost.

I must say I hand it to the jockeys. I'm told some of them make a lot of money. They deserve it. There they are, tiny little men, about half my size, on top of those enormous horses whose eyes always look dilated with rage and whose nostrils puff out great gusts of steam; then they race off like express trains, except they're not running on the rails and the riders bob up and down on the horses' backs like yoyos. If they happened to get out of time with the horses' backs, they could do themselves a terrible injury. No, I reckon they earn what they get. No money on earth would induce me to do it.

Going to the paddock is quite something; anyway it is at Ascot and Goodwood. At Epsom for some reason they keep it about a quarter of a mile's journey from the enclosure so it needs stamina to get there.

The atmosphere around the paddock is in complete contrast to that in the enclosures. There is an overall quietness. People talk, if not in whispers, in low confidential voices. They stand staring at the horses going round, occasionally pointing a finger at some feature and looking for all the world as if they knew everything there was to know about horseflesh. After hearing such learned talk about fetlocks, withers and stance, you'd imagine that they could accurately forecast the result of each race. But they can't. Well, that's obvious, isn't it? Otherwise they'd be able to pick all the winners, the bookies would be bankrupt and horses' merits would be judged at some sort of Miss World Competition on looks alone. Similarly, it's funny how people who a few minutes ago were glibly handing out tips straight from the horse's mouth are almost tongue-tied when faced with the beasts themselves. One young girl at Goodwood unconsciously called her father's bluff: 'Look, Daddy,' she said, 'there's the one you backed. Why do you think he's better than the others?' Daddy, I noticed, went slightly puce, swallowed once or twice, and then said, 'Come on, or we shall miss seeing the race.'

We're all a lot of hypocrites really, we like to be thought experts – like chaps who go around with members' tickets strung on to their binocular straps, and just want to be seen to be seasoned racegoers. Poppycock. It's like those airline bags – you don't have to have travelled by air to have one, you can buy them at Woolworth's.

Inside the paddock of course stand the owners and trainers looking self-conscious, and the jockeys looking bored; if I'd been a jockey I'd have been looking scared stiff. The owners and trainers shuffle from foot to foot, or squat on their shooting-sticks trying to think of something to say to each other.

The only exception to this that I saw was the Royal Family. At Ascot the Queen Mother had a horse running. During her spell in the paddock she carried on an animated conversation with charm and friendliness, and seemed to include everyone around in her circle.

At Goodwood the Queen had a runner in the big race. She, Prince Philip, Prince Charles and Princess Anne seemed to take over the whole paddock; all eyes were on them, yet they might have been standing in their garden at Sandringham – everyone was completely natural. They chatted, joked and laughed with each other and with their trainers and jockey. Here I could think of them as ordinary human beings. Not so when I was at Ascot watching their drive from Windsor Castle, down along the course in front of the grandstands in their open horse-drawn carriages. This was royalty on display. This was what we pay for; and it's money well spent. All right, waves and smiles came from the carriages but there was a feeling of separation. 'That is the Queen,' a voice said inside me. 'She is different from you and those around. She symbolizes what is good about this country, so forget what's wrong with it.' And along with all the others, I cheered and cheered; my eyes filled with tears, I was proud to be British.

I thought afterwards I must have been mad. It was just like a drug. I felt I wasn't the sort of person who should feel like that – feel that as long as we have a Royal Family with such grace and charm nothing very dreadful can happen to us. But, remembering the occasion now, I feel the same way. Curious.

Walking back to the enclosures after visiting the paddock, you come right down to earth again. The nearer it gets to the start of the race, the louder the bookies cry and the general hustle and excitement builds up. The tick-tack men flay the air. For all the world they look like those Indian gods who've got a dozen arms. What I missed at all the meetings was the tipsters; I could understand them not being in the Members' Enclosures, but my escort and I did wander around and we didn't see any. It always amazed me that punters bought their tips. It is obvious to me that if the tipsters had any true inside information they would be making a fortune for themselves, not for the public.

I shall always remember one, Prince Monolulu, who seemed to be at every race-meeting. Once when Albert and I went to the Derby we took our young son Harry with us. He was about six at the time and we ran into this Prince Monolulu shouting about how he'd got a horse. He was a large coloured man with a bright, flowing native dress, a crimson satin cloak and a feathered head-band, just like a Red Indian. He stooped down in front of Harry and asked him if he'd like a horse. I thought Harry would be frightened of him. He wasn't. He said yes he would and put his arms round Prince Monolulu's neck. This delighted the Prince. He stood up with him and walked around saying that Harry was his mascot for the next race and how Harry had told him what was going to win. 'Out of the mouths of babes and sucklings,' he shouted, 'comes a horse!' Everyone laughed and he did a brisk trade.

He gave us the tip for nothing. We backed it and it won! We saw him again later. I think he must have been looking for us because he handed Harry a stick of rock and two of his feathers. It was that sort of thing that used to make a day's racing for me.

The bookmakers, I'm glad to say, are still there, and much the same as they always were. Despite the growth of the totalizator, which they say is ruining their business, bookmakers always look prosperous.

I've never fancied the tote. It seems out of place on a racecourse. It's like giving your money to the nationalized industries. Far too clinical. You go up to one window, hand over your money and get a flimsy piece of paper like a savings certificate. That in itself is slightly ironic. If by chance you win you queue up at another window, present your certificate which you now feel is like your old-age-pension claim, and get your money in exchange. No, give me private enterprise every time. Bookies are real people, not just faces at the window. They're twice as large as life but that's a treat in this day of small people protecting smaller images.

Bookies trade on the desire in nine people out of ten to get something for nothing. It's called human nature, though I think it's human stupidity – so do the book-makers, but they encourage it because it's on this that they thrive. Talk about hope springing eternal in the human breast. People must know that the bookmakers win. Otherwise how could they live, and live well? But they go on subscribing to them. It's the same with the

Pools; we know there's only a million-to-one chance of any of us ever winning, but when it's published in the paper that a gas fitter or a bus driver won thousands of pounds, we think, 'Ah, someone like me won the pools, so there is no reason why I shouldn't win.' Yet if we stop to think we know that there is only a millionth of a chance.

Bookmakers are there to stop us thinking, or rather to make us think their way – that they are there to help us to realize our 'something for nothing' dream. They do this well. They reel off gay badinage, exude bonhomie, and lead you to think that their purpose in life is to be your benefactor. They've got names that inspire faith and trust, like Honest John Smith, Charlie Brown and Joe Bloggs, names you can rely on. They always look cheerful, particularly when they're forced to keep your money.

At all three meetings they were forced to keep mine. Mind you, on each occasion I played into their hands because when I put money on a horse I want a lot for a little so I back the outsiders. It was just as well for the bookies that there were a few people like me about, because the favourites all seemed to win. This in itself is interesting because of the effect it has on the bookmakers. Although they must be seething with rage inside over their losses they hand over the winnings with what passes for a smile and then project themselves all over again into a possible similar situation by wooing the punter with the same banter and badinage as before.

Another reason I enjoy betting with bookies is that I can shop around for the best price, just the same as I do in the shops and supermarkets. The only difference is of course that in the latter instance I always have something to take home with me.

It is easy to see why racing is so much a part of the London Season. The horse is and always will be the best friend of the aristocracy and moneyed classes, and the race-meeting provides a setting where they can display their wealth and distinction. Racing is like a great big masonic club, and the fact that the Royal Family are patrons gives it the final *cachet*. But, having said that, let me hasten to add that there are many crumbs that fall from the rich man's table and these are enjoyed by more ordinary people. Indeed, if my pub is anything to go by, the greatest racing experts are to be found in the public bar of your local.

COWES WEEK

WHEN I told my mother I was going to visit Cowes during Regatta Week, she said, 'Ah, yes. What an event that was for the enjoying classes.' This is my mum's expression for what I always called the nobility and gentry. Over the years I'd got used to the expression but when she said it this time I, as it were, examined it and thought how apt it was. So many of the events of the London Season are for the 'enjoying' classes. People who are able to spend their money on enjoyment and gaiety without worry. Not like most of us for whom money means food, clothing and a roof over our heads and anything left is spent after great consideration on near essentials.

What a Jekyll-and-Hyde business money is. To get it people work and scheme, jockey for position and if anyone gets in their way they brush him aside. People become selfish and self-centred in the quest for money. Yet when they spend it they become different persons – happy, hail-fellow-well-met, carefree and frivolous. Many of us have this kind of dual personality, and car drivers in particular.

Apparently in my mother's day Cowes was a very exclusive event which meant that anyone not of the aristocracy was excluded. Perhaps this was because Queen Victoria often stayed in the Isle of Wight. When I was in service it had become a more open, social occasion. None of the people I worked for had boats or yachts but they were invited by friends to enjoy the parties and balls that took place. When they came back they used to say that

Cowes wasn't what it was; that it was getting full of vulgar trippers. But they still kept going there, just as they did to Ascot, Goodwood and Henley. Yet all the time such places were becoming less exclusive. What Queen Victoria would say about the Isle of Wight and its pop festivals these days, I just shudder to think.

I'd never been on the island before. All I knew about it was what I'd got from the ladies' maids and the valets who went with the families. They spoke about the handsome naval officers in their white ducks and reefer jackets; apparently there were a number of naval ratings too because the maids spoke with relish of the junketings below decks. So the picture of Cowes that I expected was of a sort of huge promenade where the yachting enthusiasts paraded, the men in their peaked caps and blazers and the women in the latest of fashions, occasionally casting an eye out to sea to watch the yachts with their billowing sails, zooming through the ocean.

I had expected that I would get a general view of the Regatta on the ferry from Southampton to Cowes, but my escort and I travelled by Hovercraft which for someone like me who is prone to seasickness is a marvellous way of going across the water, but which gives a very restricted view of what's going on outside. So my first real glimpse of the event was the landing stage and the narrow, rather hilly streets which lead down to the promenade. I wasn't very impressed. I suppose it's a quaint little fishing-town, or was. The only evidence of fish now is the smell of frying fat that assails the nostrils from the small restaurants that line the streets. And, of course, there are the gift-shops. These were crowded with sailors, foreigners perhaps, who were looking for 'a bit of old England' to take home with them. I felt rather sad that some of these tawdry souvenirs would be exhibited in other countries as examples of British workmanship. One American sailor wanted to know if there was anything commemorating the sailing of the Plymouth Brethren. But all he got by way of an answer was, 'Oh, when was that then?'

When I got to the promenade, again I was disappointed. It's a concrete affair with iron railings near the sea, not very imposing in itself, but I had expected to see it thronged with attractive, gay, colourful people. Instead there were crowds of ordinary-looking people like myself, some massed against the railings, others wandering along in seeming aimlessness like a lot of worn-out Army recruits.

Where were the damsels and their escorts that thronged the balls each evening? I suppose the escorts might have been on the yachts crewing, or whatever it's called, and the damsels were sleeping off the rigours of the night before.

Eventually we reached the Royal Yacht Club. I'd swotted up a bit about this. It was founded in 1825 and stands on the grounds of what used to be one of Henry VIII's forts which guarded the mouth of the River Medina. Henry built twin batteries or 'cowes' either side of the river and these gave the town its name. Now one of them is the home of the most famous Yacht Club in the world. It is also, I discovered, the most exclusive. Following the old saying, 'Nothing ventured nothing gained', we tried to get in. Well, you'd have thought we were after stealing the Crown Jewels by the look on the attendant's face as he stopped us. He eyed us up and down – I thought at any moment he was going to frisk us. As we walked away I felt like something from under a stone, and my escort looked less like a 'man of the sea' than he had done previously – if that was possible.

Fortunately, for our spirits, we ran shortly afterwards into Robin Knox-Johnston whom my escort knew and we were taken off by him to the Island Sailing Club which may not be quite so exclusive as the Royal one but I reckon is all the better for that. Here you meet the real yachtsmen, and here I saw personified my earlier images of what the people at Cowes would be like. These men have an almost boyish quietness and charm of manner, yet they can break into gaiety and high spirits in less time than it takes to say Pink Gin. Robin Knox-Johnston epitomizes men of this sort: you might have expected him to be very reserved, because you think of people who can be alone for long periods at sea as introverts with lots of inner resources. But he wasn't like that at all; he was interested and interesting. I remember remarking to my escort afterwards that from talking to this world-famous man you wouldn't think he'd done any more than sail a boat along the seashore at Brighton.

By now we thought we'd better have a look at the racing. We'd already gathered that the weather was all wrong. I must say it seemed all right to us, a lovely warm summer day with none of the gales that seem to blow everlastingly on Brighton front. That, apparently, was the trouble; there was no wind to fill the sails, so everything was running behind schedule. Nevertheless, back we went along the promenade and took up our places on the rails *outside* the Royal Yacht Club.

Wordsworth said from Westminster Bridge, 'Dull would he be of soul' not to be moved by the sight he saw. I felt the same about those yachts off Cowes. Talk about 'Red Sails in the Sunset'! Here were all kinds of coloured sails and very gay they looked, even if from time to time they flapped about through lack of wind. From a distance they seemed like a bunch of coloured balloons. At first, like any housewife would be, I was a bit worried about the dye getting on to the crews' white trousers. When I remarked on this to my escort it raised quite a guffaw from other people standing by, but eventually when the laugh died down I was assured that the colours were fast and that such a calamity could not happen.

Apparently races are going on all the time. Some are over shorter distances than others, but the various types of yachts get all mixed up so the uninitiated like me don't know who is winning what when they pass the post. The winning post as you might imagine is outside the Royal Yacht Club. Now in athletics the race begins when a man fires a gun and at the end the first home breaks the tape. I never did see how they got the boats started at Cowes, but they certainly fired a gun at the end, and not just for the winner but for every boat that finishes. That's a lot of shots and a lot of noise because they don't use the ordinary pistol, they use cannon. From the look of them they might well be some of Henry VIII's left-overs. The first time one went off I nearly jumped out of my skin.

Apart from the yachts there were a lot of other ships – real ships moored off-shore. It was interesting to see the Royal Yacht *Britannia*, in the flesh as it were, for the first time. It doesn't look the least bit like a yacht, it's more like a cross-Channel steamer, though very much more romantic. I should hope so, too, because all my memories of cross-Channel steamers are of being seasick and wanting to die. Although as I say the *Britannia* is a big ship, I wouldn't fancy going around the world in it. I'd want something much larger to travel in and with a double set of stabilizers.

I looked around to see if I could find any Greek ship-owners. I expect the other debs around were too. After all, a lusty sun-bronzed handsome yachting type may be all right for a night or two but from what I've heard about the kind of money Greek shipowners have, if you manage to hook one of them you can afford to whoop it up for the rest of your life. I didn't see one but even if I had I don't suppose I'd have recognized him as such. There are a lot of bald-headed, paunchy men around who are not Greek shipowners.

I did see Prince Philip and Prince Charles. They arrived over from the *Britannia* in a launch and were duly piped ashore and hustled into the Royal Yacht Club. As usual they both looked as if they were enjoying life. I'd heard that our Prime Minister, Edward Heath, was taking part in one of the races but I didn't spot him or his yacht – which wasn't surprising seeing that he was becalmed somewhere the other side of the island. Some other boats had taken his wind, apparently. I must say when later I heard he'd been awarded the honour of Yachtsman of the Year, I was a little surprised.

During Cowes Week the pubs are open all afternoon which is nice both for visitors and locals. My escort and I joined a couple of gnarled old men at a table who soon engaged us in conversation. According to them, they were a couple of old salts, though a couple of old soaks would have been my definition. They got through three pints each at our expense within half an hour. They talked about the sea being in their bones. That's as maybe: what is certain is that alcohol was in their bloodstream. They kept on saying how if they'd only got the time they could tell us of the things they'd seen, places they'd visited, people they'd met, and all the dangers of the sailor's life in the old days. Afterwards when I came to think about our conversation they'd told us nothing except that the beer today isn't what it used to be, and I'd heard that several times before. I strongly suspect that they had never done anything more dangerous than row visitors up and down the Solent.

We took one more look at the Regatta from the promenade. There was even less wind now and the ships came limping in, giving the whole scene a rather tired air. We, too, felt it was time for home.

LUNCHING AT SIMPSON'S

To some people it may seem incongruous if not down-right odious that I dare comment on restaurant food and service, when for years my idea of lunching or dining out was a meal at Lyons. Not that I am knocking Lyons – far from it. They give quick service and hot, filling food at a price which most people can afford. And of course the people who go to expensive restaurants can't, I'm sure, use them all the time and must often be grateful for the kind of thing Lyons offer. I know I wouldn't like to use expensive restaurants all the time. It would spoil the sense of occasion and pleasurable anticipation I get when I do go to them.

Some people may wonder why I chose Simpson's as the place to lunch at during my London Season. Well, I was told that 'Simpson's in the Strand' was as much an institution as St Paul's Cathedral; that it was a place debs' dads have eaten at down the ages; and that during the Season their daughters joined them there from time to time.

There were some when I went, dressed in a variety of 'way-out' gear. Perhaps 'way-out' isn't correct, 'way-back' would be more appropriate. They wore long, straight, narrow dresses and Granny shoes or square-toed boots. When I see this heavy, restrictive clothing that women used to wear coming back, I think that the Women's Liberation Movement should start a protest in their own ranks, since their younger members at any rate look like one vast walking jumble sale.

Another thing they could turn their attention to is the way Simpson's differentiate between the sexes in favour of the male. It's 'Men Only' in the ground-floor restaurant at lunchtime. Women have to go upstairs to eat. When I tackled the Manager about this, he couldn't see why not. He said it was tradition. But then, as I told him, all tradition militated against women. I know what it dates back to: the time women were not supposed to want to lunch out. They knew their place was at home and it was for them to stay there and supervise the running of it, so that when the husband came home tired from an exhausting day in the City and a wearying three hours over lunch, willing hands lightened his cares and his wife with nothing herself to talk about was an eager listener to her husband's business chitchat. It's an absurd tradition and therefore should be done away with. I told the Manager so too. He smiled in a sort of agreement, but I know will do nothing about it.

The Manager was a Mr Mumford. He was nothing like any other restaurant manager I've ever met or spoken to. He was what I would imagine a club secretary to be, sort of warm, friendly and very proud of his place. In a way, 'club secretary' is the right description for him because when the premises were opened in 1828 it was as a chess and coffee club. A Mr Reiss was the Founder and he was joined twenty years later by Mr John Simpson, who, as it were, brought the food with him, at any rate the trolleys and the joints.

Of course, Simpson's has grown over the years but it hasn't changed, as I've said; Mr Mumford doesn't like change much, particularly in his staff. He must have the lowest staff turnover of any concern in the country. His head carver who retired a year ago had been there for fifty-one years.

Over the last hundred years there must have been few

people of importance who haven't eaten there, but there is still a hard core of regular customers – one of these has lunched there every day of the week since Mr Mumford joined the firm. Opera singers and boxers seem particularly drawn to it. I think this is because members of both professions are voracious meat eaters.

Having steeped us in History and Tradition, Mr Mumford showed us to the 'mixed' dining-room. My resentment at being treated as a mere female dissolved the moment I saw what was before me.

It was wonderful. The walls had a Wedgewood effect. There were marvellous chandeliers and well-spaced tables. I don't like places where the tables are so close together that you have to either talk in whispers or confine your remarks to comments on the weather. It's not that I want to discuss the colour problem or the Vietnam War over lunch or dinner, but I do like to gossip a bit and maybe talk about some of the people present.

I mentioned this to my escort. He said it wouldn't matter how far apart the tables were or if I spoke in a whisper because every word of what I said could be heard in the kitchen. He wasn't worried about the positioning of the tables, he was rhapsodizing over the beer. They still serve it in the old way: from barrels into copper jugs, and from the jugs into silver tankards. Apparently this means that it tastes better, but I couldn't find out why. I just got the same old answer: 'Because it's traditional.' I'd have thought the beer would get flatter by being continually transferred from one vessel to another, but then I'm a mere woman.

There's one tradition at Simpson's that I wouldn't like to see changed, and that's the service. I'd never had it so good. It was able, unobtrusive and deferential, without being servile. We were waited on by Mr Danny King who had been there for forty-five years. His father had worked there before him and so had his three brothers. From Mr King's conversation it was apparent that Simpson's was to him a way of life. During his time there he had seen some changes, but not in the standard of the food, service and surroundings. These he felt to be as good as ever. The change for him was in the customers. In his early days, lunch or dinner at Simpson's was a particular ceremony; and when I think of the vast quantity that I ate, it's one that needs regular observance – a sort of stretching of the stomach to make sure you've got room for it.

'People today,' said Mr King, 'are in too much of a hurry. They don't want to wait while a special dish is prepared. They want to eat and be off.' He mourned the leisurely way of eating. I could imagine it: courses of excellent food, erudite and witty conversation à la Oscar Wilde, washed down with a bottle of wine. Nowadays what I seem to overhear in smart restaurants is business boasting and status seeking, how equities have risen or gilt-edged have lost their gilt, and how the new Jag can do a ton in thirty seconds flat. Then, usually at about three o'clock, there comes the diatribe against the working class and its inability to do a day's work, ending with a call to the waiter: 'Four more large brandies, Harry, please.'

Recently when I was having a cup of tea and a bun in Lyons I got involved in a long and learned discussion on the industrial and social changes in Britain since the war, with a member of the so-called Hairy Brigade who quoted Toynbee and Taylor and discussed the influences of Levin and Frost on the modern scene. I've never been so entertained for 1s 6d. But I'm not going bolshie; given the choice between lunch and commonplace conversation at Simpson's or cake and culture at Lyons, I know which I'd choose.

Whenever Mr King could spare a moment he came

over to give us some more fascinating information and glimpses of the past. How during his forty-five years he had served the grandfathers and great-grandfathers of the young people who were lunching there today. How manners and behaviour developed over the years. The effect of matrimony on men. The menus he was asked to prepare for dinner parties his customers gave at home. How he advised them on their diets. When his time comes, I reckon St Peter will have him doling out the milk, honey and ambrosia for all the angels.

Mr King and the other waiters wore long, white aprons – another tradition. I suppose it was to protect their clothes in the days when buying a suit was something that was done once every ten years or so. Whatever the reason, they added an additional dignity to the waiters, and another link with the past.

But the main purpose of Simpson's is, of course, food; the chief item of which is those marvellous trolleys on which repose the superb joints of beef and saddles of mutton. These I knew were lurking on my gastronomic horizon but first I considered the sizeable list of starters. Strangely enough, I settled for soup and one with the unappetizing name of 'Thick Brown Onion'. I've always found that soup is one of the tests of a kitchen, and although many French restaurants boast about their onion soup it's seldom that you get a good one. Despite its humble name this was a superb blend of the juice of meat and onion.

Then came the trolley. You don't have to have your main course from it, but if, like me, you are sampling Simpson's for the first time I think you should. It's a gorgeous bit of pantomime to have those huge, shining containers wheeled to your table, and the treasures they contain exposed to your eyes. Then – that awful moment of choice. I hovered backwards and forwards, between sirloin of beef and saddle of mutton. I settled for the saddle and my escort had the beef. Both were superb. Incidentally, those old dinner-wagons are valuable, and plenty of Americans have offered large sums to be able to take one such home.

I thought of asking Mr King if the beef was wrapped in foil before it was cooked. It might have caused the sensation illustrated by that famous Bateman cartoon of the man who asked the carver at Simpson's if the meat was English. Today we take tinfoil for granted when cooking beef. But I often think we only really use it so that we can find the joint when we open the oven.

All Simpson's beef is bought from a farm in Scotland. It is sold to no one else. Incidentally, when Mr King started to work there the beef was three shillings per helping; now it's nineteen shillings. But it's still good value; I'd pay that to take my husband Albert there just to watch the carvers. They are a turn in themselves and an education in sheer professionalism. They should be. They start the hard way by carving for the staff. I can imagine the treatment they're given if it's not right. I must say if I worked at Simpson's I wouldn't mind getting my beef carved in chunks, it would still be tender. At home I carve my joints into rashers of wind, and they're still reminiscent of old leather.

The quantity of meat we were both given had my escort and me contemplating wrapping some up in our napkins to take home. I've gone on about the beef and haven't mentioned my saddle. Saddle of lamb or mutton is a rare dish in any home and when there are only two of you it's an unknown quantity. This is a great culinary loss and one to rectify given any opportunity. Given the opportunity of a Simpson's saddle, it would have been, I thought, 'les majesty'. I think I was right but I still get visions of that sirloin.

Nor have I mentioned the wine. I don't pretend to be a connoisseur. We consulted the wine waiter, Stanley Holmewood, another trusted employee, known as 'Granny' to the staff. He made no attempt to recommend an expensive bottle.

'If you haven't tasted our claret *en carafe*, I think you should,' was his advice. 'It is decanted at the right time and has been selected for the kind of food you will be eating.' He was quite right.

Now after two very filling courses, nobody in their right mind would have followed them as I did with tapioca pudding. Again it was in the nature of a test. Any good kitchen can turn out delectable sweets for wheeling around on a trolley, or can even make good flambeaux, but milk puddings have to be cooked and timed just right. It was worth the experiment.

It was a cream amongst milk puddings, soft and velvety. As I finished my last mouthful, my escort who was gazing at me in awe suggested I tried the boiled treacle roll. He was supported in this by Mr King who went on to tell us that there was an offer at Simpson's which had never been accepted: if after the main course anyone had eaten two slices of their treacle roll and still wanted more, he could have the third portion free.

Needless to say I refused the treacle roll but was persuaded to have a little cheese, to 'round things off'. Round things off!

'You should try the Stilton,' said Mr King, 'and, of course, a glass of our port.'

Now, ever since I was in service, I've never been able to abide Stilton. It was part of the butler's domain and the smell it made in the pantry was enough to put me off. Our butler really turned me over because when the Stilton was ripe it would get maggoty and he used to pick the maggots out with his fingers and eat them before taking the cheese upstairs.

I settled for Cheddar cheese and, of course, a glass of port. Now I've tasted some pretty good port during my time in service: 'cook's perks' it was called. But although there's a saying that stolen fruits taste sweetest, it didn't compare with Simpson's port. I had another glass as we ruminated after our meal, and was wishing the same offer applied to the port as to the treacle roll, when my escort announced he had to get back to work.

'Work'? How do men do any, after a lunch like that? I suppose it's all a question of practice. I was in a state of euphoria. I was put into a taxi, caught the train to Brighton and slept the whole way.

Reading this chapter, it does sound as if I've got shares in Simpson's. I haven't. I just didn't think places like it existed any more. Having found they do, I must speak as I found, repetitious though it may be.

One of the snags of my doing the London Season is that my husband Albert has to stay at home. He doesn't mind for most of the events but when he knows I'm going to eat and drink, well he gets a bit crochety. He always wants to hear what I've had, though. I must say he brightened considerably when I said, 'Oh, just soup, mutton, tapioca pudding and cheese.'

THE ART WORLD

I'VE always been a culture vulture. I've also realized how lucky I've been to live in Britain where there is so much to feed on, either free or for very little money. The British, though, are funny about their culture. They're almost ashamed of it. In fact, though it is their main hidden asset and makes quite a difference to the balance of payments, they resent having to maintain it financially. We pour out money to teach people when they're young, forgetting that school is only the grass roots and that education is what you do with your schooling later in life. Culture though is not a sacred cow. It's fun. Fun to enjoy and fun to criticize. It's a part of life. The London Season demonstrates this, and I enjoyed this part of it as much as any.

Technically, the Season begins I believe with the Private Viewing of the Royal Academy Summer Exhibition. My escort tried to get invitations for the viewing, but, having failed, wasn't sufficiently well-informed to be able to arrange for us to gatecrash, for which I am heartily grateful. I found it hard enough to concentrate on the pictures, going as I did a few days later. From what I've heard of Opening Day, it's like a fancy-dress show at the Zoo and any resemblance of the guests to the human species is entirely coincidental.

Although throughout my life I've tried to understand and appreciate art I've never really succeeded. 'I know what I like' is a cliché which can be applied to me; but

99

since my early married life was spent in Chelsea I suppose I wanted to be able to like what those around me seemed to enjoy, to widen my area of appreciation. I did in literature. I don't think I have with fine art. I visited art galleries a lot when I was in service, on my days off, but that was either to get out of the rain or on the chance of meeting some intelligent young man; so my concentration was not on the exhibits. Nevertheless, I think I have a more than average curiosity and interest in painting and painters.

I think the first time I became conscious of the attraction of pictures was in my first job as a kitchenmaid. I had the house more or less to myself first thing in the morning when I was cleaning the hall and the front steps. There was a large oil painting facing the front door of some distinguished-looking old buffer, probably an ancestor of the family I was working for. Very stern-looking he was, and his eyes sort of followed me wherever I went. At first he almost frightened me, and I felt he was criticizing the way I was doing my work. But I got over this and eventually I became quite friendly with him. We used to have little chats together. I remember once, when I was polishing the floor, I swivelled round on my knees, my skirt came up over my behind and as I turned round to adjust it I swear there was a twinkle in his eyes. 'You dirty old man,' I chuckled at him. It's just as well nobody else was about. To have been caught talking to a picture! Still, I had to do something to make menial work tolerable, didn't I?

Ever since I can remember reading about it, the Royal Academy Summer Exhibition has been a target for adverse criticism but then anything to do with fine art suffers from this. There seem to be no criteria of what is good or bad. It's a matter of opinion. This is true of other arts, but to a much smaller degree. Any statue sculpted or portrait painted of anyone living or in living memory raises a storm of controversy which becomes national news. But when the experts are asked to pass judgement and to justify their opinions, they either waffle or else talk in a technical jargon which is incomprehensible to anyone who's not a specialist, and I suspect often incomprehensible to those who are.

I can read theatrical or literary criticism and understand what the play or book is about, and sometimes whether I am likely to enjoy it. Art criticism does nothing to interest or help me.

It is this looseness of judgement, I think, that has robbed the Academy of the authority it once had. It has meant that a strong personality has been able to dominate the indecisiveness of others so that its selection appears dogmatic and reactionary. This hasn't altogether been a bad thing since painters who have had their work rejected have been able to take the rebuff as a compliment and continue working unperturbed, but it has affected the public's attitude towards art and those whom they consider to be the authorities on art.

From what I saw this year there seems to have been a great change. There was something of everybody's for everybody. In fact it seemed to me that the pendulum had swung too far and that to counter the accusations of being too conformist, some paintings that lacked any artistic merit had been chosen simply because they were unconventional. There was a quota of pictures like 'Rough Sea at Brighton', 'The Harbour, Dunkirk' and such like; there were the usual still lifes, nudes and portraits of officials looking as self-opinionated as a Birmingham councillor about to watch a film on sex education. But there were others more challenging. One I saw was just a door in a room, yet it radiated a feeling of mystery. It could have led anywhere and it aroused in my mind all sorts of images. Another, which I think should hang in every nuclear scientist's sitting-room as a sort of conscience tickler, showed how the world would look after an atomic explosion. There was another next to it whose title I don't recall, but which I christened 'Intestines' – just the thing to empty a doctor's surgery. Another was actually called 'Implosion' – a word I've never come across before – sort of green and blue eggs on a dark mauve background. All right, I suppose, if you like your eggs that colour. Then there were a number with the coloured squares, triangles and circles which completely defeat me – sort of Euclid without the '*quod erat demonstrandum*'.

But taking them all in all I enjoyed them. There was plenty of contrast and the Exhibition was, I think, an indication of what is going on in the art world, and it was entertaining. The arrangement of the galleries was good, though I must say I could have done with more seats. You do need to take the weight off your feet pretty often in a picture gallery.

An interesting comparison I was able to make was of behaviour patterns. When I first started going into galleries, people used to shuffle past the nudes. Some women would blush, others in pairs would snigger. None would stop and enjoy the body beautiful.

Today there are no such inhibitions. Our senses have been so assaulted going up escalators or walking past a cinema that we are now able to enjoy a painting or drawing of the human form divine without embarrassment, though I still feel there are very few people who don't look better wearing some clothing. Some men seemed to me to be peering too close for decency, and I don't think they were just studying the brushwork.

The atmosphere at the Tate Gallery was in contrast to that at the Academy. People it appeared were there to see, not just to be seen. Parties of earnest people were being escorted round the gallery by equally earnest guides giving a blow-by-blow account of the pictures. I tagged on to one of these parties, thinking that I would improve my education and pick up a pointer or two.

Now I know 'life is real, life is earnest', but it doesn't have to be that way for me in an art gallery. Leave me alone with my 'empty dreams' and let me fill them my own way and in my own time. I don't like the kind of cultural forced feeding that these guides inflict on you. In any case I don't believe the guff they give forth. They try and psychiatrize the dead: 'This was his dark period, the time when his wife had left him for Count Reynard, his mistress had whooping cough and his passion for the local butcher was not reciprocated. It affected his brush-work.' Codswallop! People have to dream up an explanation for everything. Artists have to have a perpetual sense of purpose. They're not allowed to paint because they enjoy it or because they need the money. In any case who cares what the artist was thinking about at the time? And surely art can be inconsequential and gay and still be good.

I think the thing that finally made me break away from my 'cultural', escorted group was when a woman asked what price a particular picture would fetch today and was it fashionable art? What an appalling yardstick to have to apply. Yet it's the common one. Take this new expression 'trendy'. It means 'Yeah, it's good. I like it because everybody else likes it.' We're afraid today to have an opinion. Then there are the inflated prices that people pay for pictures, not because they think of them as things of beauty and a joy for ever, but because they consider them a good investment in an unstable financial world. Also it gives them a social importance which they are unable to get any other way.

Having left my escorted group I was alone with my catalogue. This I found presented certain difficulties since it used phrases to describe the pictures that added to my difficulty in understanding them.

I mean, how do expressions like 'bulbous tapering features' or 'metamorphic meanings' or 'an unprejudiced approach to the objective world' help to lighten the intellectual load? Who do they write these catalogues for? Are they for people who already know? If so, they needn't bother. If they're for the uninformed like me who have no idea what a 'metamorphic meaning' and a 'tapering bulbous feature' are, then they're wasting their time. I reckon when a catalogue is as obscure as the things it's trying to describe we're really in trouble. So I gave up consulting it and let my imaginative powers take over. They found the next picture I looked at to be a number of pipes running along the Underground except that they were blue. A collection of different-sized, highly coloured squares by Matisse, my imaginative powers thought were a collection of different-sized highly coloured squares by Matisse. A picture called 'Painting' left them standing. They reckoned the artist called it that because he couldn't remember what it was or why he'd ever done it.

I think my imaginative powers must be pretty old because these sorts of things seemed to enthral younger people. I noticed how two young men were sitting and gazing at a large expanse of alternate green, white and blue lines and when I came back half an hour later they were still deep in contemplation of them. I wanted to tell them that they could buy wallpaper just like that and sit at home and gaze at it for eternity.

I overheard a girl describe it as a 'fun' picture, but whether she meant it was fun for the painter or viewer I didn't like to ask.

It may seem as if for me the visit to the Tate was a waste of time. It wasn't – I loved the Turners, the Stubbses and the Constables and I spent a lot of time with them. These are the kind of works that I would like on the walls of my home. To people who know that I am not really a lover of nature this choice of mine may seem strange, but you don't have necessarily to be a lover of nature to enjoy them. Just as I agree with Anthony Powell that 'books do furnish a room', so I believe that pictures do as well. But pictures with colours that shriek at you and shapes that suggest immediate calamity could only make a madhouse. As for Pop Art I think it's done just to shock you. I don't want to be shocked by a painting. Life has enough shocks during the course of an ordinary day.

How can a layman know what is true or false art when a painting of a can of soup is said to be worth £25,000? We are told to make up our minds whether it is sublime or ridiculous. We are advised by an eminent Art Critic to 'let all our preconceived notions of art die so that we can live in the real world of contemporary art'. To me it's all a maze. I am lost and it seems there is no one to guide me to a proper understanding and appreciation.

Take the last exhibit I looked at: several planks of green wood were interlaid with black poles. It was on the floor, of course. It couldn't be put anywhere else. To me it was neither functional nor beautiful, and it certainly wasn't a space saver. Yet two people were looking at this collection of flotsam and jetsam admiringly and caressing it with remarks like 'What vision, what vitality!' I can only think that something's gone wrong with my aesthetic education, but I'm not sure that I want to put it right.

THE ROYAL OPERA

UNTIL the night I went to the Opera, Covent Garden for me was a vegetable market where the pubs opened very early in the morning. I got this last piece of information from my friend Vi, who was evacuated from Stepney to Hove during the war and who came to live next door. Like me she did charring jobs, and had done most of her married life. At some time she'd worked for a fruit-and-veg merchant. 'A very frisky gent' she described him as. Apparently he used to get up early in the morning and drive off to Covent Garden, returning home around eight o'clock, when Vi was starting work, and he always came back in a very merry mood which, as Vi said, wasn't natural in a man. Nor was it natural for a woman to have to fend for her honour at that time of the day.

'I had to leave making the beds till he went back to work at nine,' Vi told me. 'He was a very slippery customer and if he ever caught me bending it was a hard struggle. When I told him it wasn't right to feel like that at that hour of the morning, he would roar with laughter and blame the strong coffee he got at the Garden. I'll say it was strong coffee,' Vi went on, 'so bloody strong the fumes would nearly put me under and I'd almost give up struggling. I dare say if he'd brought me a drink back I might have surrendered, but he never did. Too bloody mean, and I wouldn't give an inch to a mean man.' Then she roared with laughter.

Despite the fact that the market was closed when we

went to the Opera, it was still very much in evidence. The smell of fruit and veg pervaded everywhere, and since my escort and I couldn't get a taxi and had to go by Tube, the walk to the theatre gave us the opportunity of studying as well as smelling its environs. I reckon it's still very much the same as it was at the time Bernard Shaw wrote *Pygmalion*, and not what you'd expect for the setting of an Opera House of the highest international standing. In a way, though, I'm glad we had that walk because the contrast on entering the theatre is breathtaking. I've never been inside a more beautiful place. It was dazzling. The tiers were a blaze of light and the chandeliers seemed to be dripping sunshine. I could imagine what such surroundings and jewels would do for ladies in their silks and satins, with their diamond tiaras. On this occasion everyone was in mufti as it were.

When I was in domestic service I remember the families setting off for the Opera: the ladies done up to the nines in their elaborate dresses, mink coats and wraps, wearing as much jewellery as they could hang on themselves, withdrawn by the master of the house with much ceremony and clanking of the keys from the safe near the butler's pantry; the men in their tails, opera cloaks and hats, carrying black, silver-topped canes. They would set off to the accompaniment of 'oohs' and 'aahs' from the above-stairs servants; and the grumbles of the cook in the kitchen preparing the repast for their return. And what a supper they came back to. None of your already-cut-up bits and bobs and tins of this and that, which passes for a cold meal today. There would be smoked salmon sides, whole fresh salmon, lobster, caviare, game pies – you name it, it was there; and the butler busying himself with the wines and champagnes and cigars. What a to-do it was. I enjoyed watching and helping in the preparation, but I felt differently when it came to clearing and washing up afterwards. I would stagger up to bed at about two in the morning, asleep on my legs, and with the knowledge I'd got to be up again by six.

I was given a picture or two of what went on upstairs by the housemaids and was occasionally able to steal a glimpse myself. The women opera singers were big and full-chested; their men were various shapes and sizes but always, it seemed, rotund. Both sexes had voices that used to make the glasses ring. They used them as though they were trying to ensure that the back row could hear as well as the front. Something to do with throwing the voice and resonance, or so I was told when I went to speech classes as a part of my public-speaking lessons. A lot of it is in the breathing. I used to do exercises for ten minutes each morning, breathing in and counting out. Albert didn't care for it. He said that I'd got enough voice without disturbing the whole street.

Anyway, apart from having big voices these opera singers had big appetites. They went through cook's efforts like a plague of locusts. With this kind of supper we used to hope for a few perks afterwards below stairs but they always finished everything. I've learnt since that opera singing takes a lot out of you physically. I must say their jaws worked overtime putting a lot back in again.

Contraltos, in my young days at any rate, seemed to be the biggest of women. One of the ladies in a house I worked in when I was thirteen was a contralto. She used to practise while I was cleaning around; very soulful songs she'd sing. There was one about a lover who'd strayed instead of carrying off the heroine to live happily ever after. How he could really have been expected to lift some fourteen stone of her was a mystery to me. I remember thinking how different the tone she used for singing was compared with the one she used when she spoke to me. Her bosoms seemed to do a lot of the work for her, and she had a lot of bosom. 'Rocked in the Cradle of the Deep' was a favourite of hers. I don't know about 'cradle of the deep', she had a cleavage like a mineshaft!

The opera we went to see was Mozart's *The Marriage of Figaro*. A few nights before I was a guest at a sherry party, and I mentioned as a conversational gambit my forthcoming visit. I wished I hadn't. It soon became obvious that I was the only one in the room who didn't know anything about it. Apparently Mozart was *the* composer of opera – a purist, no one could compare with him; Verdi, Gluck and Rossini couldn't hold a candle to him. I was treated to a list of his operas that I ought to see and obviously he'd written a lot. I tried to swing the conversation in another direction. The only thing I'm a real expert in is cooking, and it's hard to stop an opera fanatic in full flight by talking about Béarnaise Sauce, or even Beef Strogonoff. At last in desperation I said I didn't think I really cared for opera. That really put the cat among the pigeons.

'Not care for opera? You can't mean it! Not real opera? Not Mozart. Everyone loves Mozart.'

That was the end for me. I shut up like a clam. Why do people make these sweeping statements when it's obvious there must be millions of people who've never even heard of Mozart, or indeed of any classical composer, and couldn't care less if they never do. I must say you could have included me on that particular evening.

The Marriage of Figaro was sung in Italian. I suppose the nature of the opera doesn't lend itself to the English language. All that intrigue, jealousy and passion is alien to us. In Britain, if love doesn't run smoothly we shrug our shoulders and look around for somebody else. It was supposed to be a comedy but nobody in the audience laughed. I suppose opera is a sacred cow and not meant to be laughed at. To my mind, *The Marriage of Figaro* was like a pantomime for grown-ups, a timeless story with the chief character behaving as though he suffered from paranoia.

The story follows on from an opera of Rossini's, *The Barber of Seville*. The Count has now married the Countess and she is very much in love with him, but he is a man who likes to have something on the side. He fancies Susanna, one of the maids who is engaged to a manservant, Figaro – but she's all for keeping it for her intended. Then there's a page who's after the Count's wife; she's a sort of principal boy in the pantomime, a woman dressed in man's clothing, which doesn't make things easier for following the story.

The Count finds the Page in the Countess' bedroom and so he gets all jealous – which goes to show how inconsistent men are. Well, it's a mass of intrigue, with everybody seeing everybody else in the garden by dressing up in each other's clothes. And it all happens in one day, the day of Susanna's wedding. Which shows how immoral the Italians are. Any British nobleman would have waited a week or two until Susanna was tiring of her husband before making a bid for her.

The extraordinary thing is that having said what I've said about opera, I must confess that after a certain initial shock I found myself enjoying it. I began to think that I was more intellectual than I'd given myself credit for. In fact I could now imagine myself taking the dominant rôle in any future discussion on the opera. I often get these delusions. I'm like a female Walter Mitty.

In the next interval we went into the Crush Bar where I did a bit of listening in to other people's conversations. I'd noticed a party of young people two rows in front of us, and I'd watched their faces from time to time during the opera. They had sat in rapt attention and I'd thought what a charming, intellectual set they were. In the bar, they really let their hair down. They sent the opera up rotten and started flirting quite violently in front of everybody. They fairly got the cold shoulder from the more elderly. One forbidding lady, who looked every inch a dowager duchess, curled her lip and said, 'Isn't it sad how Covent Garden has changed? When I first came here it was all so different and so dignified. When I was a girl we behaved with respect and were treated with respect. Now the place is little better than the market. Anything goes.'

I don't agree. In her day her society was littered with sacred cows, and any kind of criticism, or non-acceptance, was considered as profanity. Just because those youngsters didn't discuss the opera as if it was some divinely inspired writing, like the Dead Sea Scrolls, didn't mean that they were not interested, and just because they behaved a bit amorously didn't mean that they were inhabitants of Sodom and Gomorrah.

Mind you, this acceptance of the decrees and opinions of our elders and betters was not confined to high society. I remember one butler I used to work under. He was a prosaic character who often uttered some ancient aphorism as though it was a pearl beyond price. Whenever he read some startling piece of news that he didn't understand, he remarked ponderously, 'I don't believe all the stuff they print nowadays.' And we all used to nod our heads in agreement and murmur, 'How right you are,' although privately we thought him a bore and a humbug.

Like so many of the things that make up the London Season, going to the opera is an event in the real sense of the word. The grand surroundings, the sense of the past, and the music all contribute to the enjoyment of the evening. But I must admit that the end of the evening seemed rather an anti-climax, and when I arrived back home in the early hours of the morning I decided to get the taxi to take me on to my mother's flat. I knew that she would still be awake as, being ninety now, she needs little sleep. Although my mother likes her flat I can't help feeling that the authorities showed a lack of tact when they sited the mortuary at the end of the road – especially as the flats are for old people only. My mother, who talks of dying as most people talk about shopping, says when she feels her time has come she's going to walk along to the mortuary and just lie down. 'It will save everybody a lot of trouble.'

She was delighted to see me at one-thirty in the morning; but far from wanting to hear about my night at the opera she reminisced about the grand entertaining that used to go on in 1895 when she was a kitchenmaid. It all seemed a great contrast to my mother's life now in her two-roomed flat.

The following day I was invited by a television company to give my reactions to the opera; some people must have been interested in them or I wouldn't have been asked to appear. But my mother certainly hadn't been. I couldn't help feeling that a mother is a great head-shrinker. It is her 'You just listen to me, my girl!' that will prevail between us as long as she lives.

THE RUSSIAN BALLET

I WAS introduced to ballet when I was in service. The daughters and sometimes grand-daughters of the house used to have lessons in the art. It was the nanny's or under-nurse's job to take them to their classes once a week, and they never seemed to enjoy it.

'A lot of footling nonsense,' one nanny described it to me. 'There they stand holding on to a bar and twisting their feet into different positions; it isn't natural. Nor is it right them standing on their toes,' she went on. 'Makes them deformed. As for the dancers themselves, I don't think even the teacher knows what they're getting at. There's no rhyme nor reason in them at all. And all this dressing up, just makes the children into conceited little madams.'

Well, I didn't comment. The trouble with nannies was that they'd say one thing one minute and another the next, and they were always likely to repeat anything that came from the servants' hall to them upstairs.

I remember how on some nights after dinner the children would be brought down dressed in their tights and frilly skirts, the piano would start to tinkle and they'd do their little dances for the guests. Then there'd be the usual polite handclaps, the 'Isn't she sweet's', the 'Charming's', the 'Goodnight, darling's', and off they'd troop to bed. Then we'd have a go in the kitchen, a much more spirited affair than upstairs, ending with the parlour-maid and I twirling around with our skirts billowing out showing our coloured garters. 'Charming,' the butler would say at the end, but in a different tone of voice.

Since then I've never felt drawn to the ballet. I've seen it on television but it didn't seem to me to lend itself to the medium. The screen's too small; you are given either just one or two dancers away from the general scene, or the sort of view that you get when you look through the wrong end of a telescope. I never stayed with it long on the telly. However, I could see that it fitted in as part of my London Season.

Since I'd been to the opera at Covent Garden, I took the opportunity of varying the locale and visiting the Royal Festival Hall during the Russian Ballet season. This was the first time I'd been inside it. Like any new building, painting or sculpture, there had been a lot of criticism about it. People said it was too way out and it didn't harmonize with its surroundings. Remembering what was there before, I couldn't see what the fuss was about. Did people want it to harmonize with Waterloo Station and County Hall? I reckon it's an expression of its age and a pleasant one at that. Mind you, I suppose you could call the Shell building an expression of its age. A very nasty expression at that. How the authorities allowed that monstrosity must be beyond human comprehension.

I'd heard that inside the Festival Hall you get perfect acoustics. I don't know about that but I do believe the interior to be a real work of art. There is the most dramatic effect of space as you walk in, and the seating is arranged so that everyone has an uninterrupted view of the stage. The air-conditioning gives a constant feeling of freshness. And the boxes! They must give a wonderful view, though I'm not sure that I'd like to sit in one; they seem to be suspended in mid-air.

Now of course comes the crunch. What effect did the

ballet performance have on me? I consider myself to be a fairly intelligent person, but as far as ballet is concerned I flatter myself. It completely baffled me. What does it mean? I expected it to appeal to my senses. I hoped to be enthralled, caught up with the movement and spectacle, transported to another level of emotional experience. I'd heard it was exotic and sensual. It did nothing for me. It was as lifeless as frozen cod on the fishmonger's slab. To me the dancers were as moving icicles, like the figures on a Grecian vase – a form of art that has never aroused me. I expected to get some sort of reaction at any rate from the male dancers – but who can get excited about a man romping about in a skintight corset?

Apparently there are a lot of people who can. It was obvious from the rapt attention around me that I was a minority of one. Everyone seemed utterly oblivious to anything except the dancers. As a rule one can divide a theatre audience into three groups. The genteel elderly who go to every new show as a matter of habit and routine. The well-to-do who make it an evening out either for the wife or the girlfriend. They do it with a large box of chocolates, and the play is often spoiled for those around by their whispered conversation punctuated with the rustling of chocolate papers. Then there are the true theatre-goers who go when through their inside knowledge they know that the play will be worth seeing.

At the ballet everyone seemed to be dedicated to the art. In an interval I talked to a young man who was a real ballet fan. Whenever possible, he spent every evening going to the ballet. I'd have thought that knowing exactly what was coming next would have taken the enjoyment away, but he assured me that he enjoyed ballets more at each performance. He was completely unable to understand my philistine attitude, but then I can't understand why people don't enjoy a good play or a good book.

I'm prepared to admit that there's something wrong with me; but I'm not prepared to believe that half the people who go to ballet understand it. I think they go because it is the thing to do.

It seems to me you want a complete knowledge of the human anatomy, because how can you appreciate the movements of arms and legs of a dancer if you don't know their normal limitations? Then there's a kind of ballet language so that through movement the story is expressed. How do you study this? What makes you want to? I most certainly was completely at sea as to what the dances were about, even though I'd read the programme notes. The only conclusion I can reach is that it's something for young people – by that I mean something you've got to start going to when you're young. It's hard at my age to accept new conventions in art.

Another thing that disturbed me was the applause that kept interrupting the performance. For example, in 'Aurora's Wedding' as soon as the Blue Birds began leaping around and defying the laws of gravity, the audience started to clap and cheer. In fact whenever there was any prodigious feat during the evening, the audience sort of burst in. I found it disrupted my attempted stream of thought; and heaven knows, I was finding it hard enough to concentrate and not start preparing the menu for tomorrow's dinner. After all, dancing is a collective thing, it's not just individuals giving a variety turn. In any case, green though I am to it all, I would have thought that many of the less spectacular steps were probably the more difficult ones and that real ballet experts would know this instead of always applauding the pyrotechnics of the stars. I'm not sure that it wasn't the audience trying to show how knowledgeable they were. A sort of intellectual one-upmanship.

I left the Festival Hall sadder, but none the wiser. It

isn't as if I don't like dancing. I was a devotee when I was younger, and on the films I've always enjoyed watching Fred Astaire, Gene Kelly and their partners. I could understand and appreciate them, but to see women cavorting around on one leg like flamingoes or men leaping into space like herons – well, for me it's best left to the birds.

STRATFORD-ON-AVON

IT may seem to be a bit strange to include a visit to Stratford-on-Avon in my London Season but I was given to understand that nowadays there are quite a few intellectual young girls for whom a visit there is considered a must.

Anyway, when I had the opportunity I jumped at it. Not that I consider myself in any way intellectual, but I do like Shakespeare. Why this is I don't know because I suffered a very rough passage with him when I was at school. He and I were introduced when I was about twelve by our class teacher, Miss Taylor, a spinster of some fifty years. I liked this Miss Taylor; but she was always going on about how she'd come down in the world, though in my eyes and those of the other girls she was in comparative heaven. This was because she was always wearing something new, whereas we were in cast-offs.

A number of us had a crush on her. She seemed to like this, and would frequently be inviting one or two of the girls round to her flat for tea on a Sunday afternoon. These favoured ones used to tell us later of all the good things they had had to eat, but when we pressed for information on what went on after tea the girls would become evasive and hint at events far beyond our comprehension.

I was one of the last to be asked and to achieve the goal I had to become a nauseating sycophant for weeks. The tea wasn't a success. I was completely overawed by my surroundings. It was a lush sort of room, dramatically furnished with chaise-longues and silk cushions, and lit with shaded lamps. There were books all up the walls. 'I love books, don't you, Margaret?' Miss Taylor said. Well, as we'd got only about half a dozen at home, I didn't know what to say. I only knew that I liked reading. This got me off on the wrong foot; all my inferiority feelings came over me and I was practically tongue-tied for the rest of my visit, murmuring 'Yes, Miss' and 'No, Miss' from time to time and leaving the rest of the conversation to her.

Whenever we had tea at home we all sat up at the kitchen table, but at Miss Taylor's I sat doing a juggling act with a cup of tea in one hand and a plate in the other. This made me even more nervous. The tea-cup started to rattle away in the saucer and it seemed as if the sound filled the whole room. Eventually the inevitable happened and I spilled the tea over one of the silk cushions. I get hot flushes now when I think of it. After I'd tried mopping it up as best I could, I beat a hasty retreat.

I was never asked again and I don't believe it was because I stopped being sycophantic. I think really that Miss Taylor was a kind woman, because I remember shortly after this she was standing over my desk looking at my work, and she put her arm round me. Now in our family, and I think in most working-class families, there was never very much outward show of affection so that one grew to dislike it. I suppose it was looked on as a sign of weakness. Anyway, I immediately sort of edged away from her and I think this created the final barrier between us. That and *Midsummer Night's Dream*.

Miss Taylor was very fond of this play and we often read it in class. Then it was decided that we would act certain scenes in front of the rest of the school. I was cast

119

as Bottom. Now I know it's a leading part so I ought to have been pleased, but when I was twelve it was also physically my leading part – one I was being reminded of constantly at home and at school – so I didn't want anything to happen that would attract greater attention to it. Within a few hours, of course, the whole school knew of my fate. I was never able to live it down. Nor did I feel like giving the rôle the attention it deserved. Everyone found the idea funny enough without my adding any additional comic business.

I thought my cup of bitterness was full when I was given the ass' head to wear at rehearsals. But worse was to follow. The part of Titania, queen of the fairies, had been given to Miss Taylor's pet, a girl called Esmeralda. She was a pretty little thing with long flaxen hair which when it wasn't plaited came down to her knees. She had to suffer a bit as well as me because 'Titania' has a fairly obvious abbreviation. Anyway, Titania in one scene gets a crush on Bottom because someone squeezes the juice of a flower over her, so Esmeralda and I had to spend some time in close proximity. Came the day when we were to perform the piece, and Esmeralda turned up minus her golden locks. They'd all been shorn off because she'd got lice or nits.

Well, sorry though I was for poor Esmeralda, I was sorrier still for myself. I'd got to lie in this close proximity with her and I could imagine her livestock transferring themselves to my head. That day was one of the most disastrous in my life. The play was a dismal failure. There were some laughs but generally in the wrong places. When I left school it was to a chorus of braying from the playground and when I got home and told Mum what had happened, my head was anointed with Percipity powder mixed with lard, as a precaution against the lice, and I was shunned for days by my brothers and sisters.

That Shakespeare survived such a disastrous introduction must surely be a tribute to his works. He has survived because I've read most of his plays and his sonnets, and am what you call a Shakespeare fan.

I'd never before made the pilgrimage to the shrine at Stratford though. I had arranged to meet my escort there, so I went by train. The station is a nice distance from the town. So often some of our most beautiful and interesting towns are bisected by the railway and spoiled because of it. At first sight Stratford seems like a bright clean English market town. The evidences of Shakespeare's association with it are not particularly apparent until you seek them out. Once you get to the river, you find it's dominated by the Theatre which I believe when it was built aroused a lot of architectural criticism, but which now seems to blend in with its surroundings and the backcloth of Holy Trinity Church. There is always some critic to carp at any modern public building; they love to tell you how the architect's dream has turned into a nightmare. I think it's a pity these critics don't concentrate on some of the hideous blocks of flats going up; then perhaps they might stop putting up these 'towers of loneliness'.

I met my escort at the hotel we were staying in by the river. It was a pleasant place, comfortable without being pretentious and comparatively inexpensive, but my spirits dropped when we went into the sitting-room – everybody looked so old. It was like a London club in the afternoon. I don't think anyone was actually sleeping, but they all looked as if they were. All right, I'm no chicken, and I know some people treat Shakespeare as a sort of god, but this seemed to be taking reverence to extremes. I adapted myself to the tone of the room and threw some conversational hisses to my escort. I knew we were going to have to have an early dinner so one of these hisses said, 'Warrabouta drink?' My escort nodded and, sidling down the aisle between the chairs, left the room. He returned about five minutes later with the hall porter carrying an ice bucket and a bottle of champagne. 'Wait for the explosion,' he whispered to me.

I looked apprehensively round at all the semi-recumbent figures. Meantime the hall porter was fidgeting with the wire round the cork of the bottle. It became apparent even to my untutored eyes that he didn't know what he was about, and that this was probably the first bottle of its kind he'd ever tried to open. He bent over to have a closer look. Suddenly my escort sprang up, grabbed the bottle and pushed the porter away. Just in time. The cork exploded from the bottle with a loud bang, missing the porter's face by inches, and part of the contents cascaded after it. The effect on the others in the room was glorious. They bounced up from their seats with shock, then down again, resumed their previous positions, and went on as though nothing had happened. A truly British reaction, I thought. This, of course, started me off laughing and as we wended our way down the bottle, the situation became more hilarious so that eventually we had to leave the room for the bar, which had now opened.

By the time we went into dinner we were both in a gay mood and indulged in a lot of light conversation and laughter during the meal. Gradually some of the faces around us began to thaw out and even to smile and laugh. Some people even started calling out to us from their tables. Eventually, the head waiter came up and thanked us, saying, 'I reckon everyone's enjoyed their meal tonight.' It's amazing what a bottle of champagne at the right time can do.

We were still in a mellow mood when we went to the theatre to see *Measure for Measure*. I liked the inside of the theatre as much as the outside. Perhaps it hasn't got the glamour of some of the older theatres, but it's so designed that you can see and hear what goes on from any seat. Those ornate neo-gothic theatres with pillars may be aesthetically pleasing but it's not very amusing to find your view obscured, and to have to keep craning your neck, to your own annoyance and that of the people behind you.

The play is not one of my favourites. It's listed as one of Shakespeare's comedies, yet the theme is the choice between Isabella, the heroine's, honour or her brother's life. Since she chooses her honour it's hardly a matter for laughter even after a bottle of champagne. Then the leading character, the Duke, creeps around in disguise trying to conduct a personal gallup poll on what the people think about the way they're governed. That's no way for a ruler to behave. Next, having made all this fuss about her virginity, the heroine throws her cap over the windmill at the end and gives it to the Duke, off-stage, of course, and after the play's over.

It seemed to me a somewhat sordid and nasty play. As usual, the critics had gone to town about it, finding allusions and meanings that perhaps even Shakespeare himself didn't know were there. It's the same whenever a new cast acts a play. Next morning the critics write reams on how this or that particular actor interpreted Hamlet or Henry. I remember reading a criticism of *King Lear*. 'The theme of Lear is an inquiry into the existence, or non-existence, of Heaven and Hell,' it said. 'Aristotelian tragedy; it purges the soul.' Well, who wants to go to the theatre to be purged? I certainly don't. But I must say I enjoyed the acting and the production. As usual Shakespeare's language and verse triumphed over the plot and I left very conscious of the excitement of good theatre.

It was a short walk to a pub called the 'Black Swan', but re-christened the Dirty Duck. Here we were given VIP treatment. I thought it must be because my escort was known there, but he modestly assured me that the same welcome is given to all old customers and friends. There was a feeling of gaiety everywhere; we had an excellent supper with some more good wine, and bubbling young company. Later we were whisked away to a party. It was in the early hours that we returned to our hotel to a rather sleepy night porter. I couldn't help feeling there was more life to be had in a short few hours at Stratford than in a week at Brighton.

Before retiring we couldn't resist another look at the hotel sitting-room, the scene of our earlier explosive entry to Stratford. Despite the fact that it was now unoccupied, in our euphoric state it was as though they were still there. We ordered a nightcap and toasted the empty chairs. Then, like Pepys, we made our ways merrily to bed.

We woke up late to a fine summer morning, ideal, as my escort said, for exploring Shakespeare's town and countryside. First to Holy Trinity. A beautiful steepled church where Shakespeare is buried, now like so many similar places in need of funds to restore it. By chance we met one of the churchwardens who kindly and proudly showed us round. But interesting though this was for me, I was more impressed by the immediate surroundings; the view from the church path by the side of the river was breathtaking. Which, for me, is saying something, because generally speaking I'm no country lover.

Then Anne Hathaway's cottage, now completely restored after a recent fire. It has been given the garden and setting that a country cottage should have and although it was late in the year the flowers added to the feeling of freshness. As we looked around we were joined by a party of Americans with badges which showed that they belonged to some Mid-West Women's Association. From their conversation which came over loud and clear they were on a Grand Tour of Europe, and were Doing Britain in Five Days. It reminded me of the time I did Cologne in half an hour, twenty minutes of which I spent queueing up for the loo!

While they were in Anne Hathaway's cottage, the word 'quaint' was very much overused. The wooden plates were 'quaint', so were the fireplaces and the carved wooden beds. One portly, over-dressed woman exclaimed, 'Gee, I really envy the people who lived in this kind of cottage. What a quiet, simple, peaceful life they must have had.' Well, this nearly started me off. You don't have to have had the lifetime of house-cleaning that I've had to realize what work and drudgery it must have been keeping a place like that clean and heated. Think of the preparing and cooking of meals with so few bowls and utensils, the fetching and carrying of water, not to speak of the kind of outdoor sanitation they had to put up with. Talk about a woman's work never being done – those were the days when that phrase was coined.

One look at this obviously well-to-do matron was enough to convince me that she had everything to make her life easy – central heating, washing machine, deep freeze, probably air-conditioning. The simple life, I thought. If anyone's got it you have. However my ruffled feathers soon fell back into place as we drove round the countryside, taking a look at Mary Arden's House, Charlecote Park, where Shakespeare is supposed to have poached deer.

Back in Stratford we looked at Shakespeare's house from the outside; we wanted to get in but so did a hundred other people. Then we wandered up the High Street, saw the timbered Almshouses, the Grammar School and Chapel and went into the New Place Gardens. Stratford has so many gardens, all beautifully and naturally laid out and so restful after the busy, crowded and noisy streets. I don't know who's responsible for the way Stratford is today. I imagine it's the Stratfordians. Those I spoke to seemed proud of their town. There is always, I think, someone who takes the lead. From chatting around one name came up fairly frequently: Flower. The Flower family. They were brewers at Stratford and still lend their name to beer. Apparently, though, for three or four generations they have influenced both the town and the theatre, and things to do with Shakespeare. They have been the connecting link and I think William himself would have liked this. I went there expecting that the Shakespeare Cult would have destroyed Stratford but it hasn't. All right, it's commercialized, but not out of recognition. The timbered buildings are picturesque and in the right setting. They are never quaint. Even where shops have taken over, the shop fronts have been left as they originally were.

Of course there are places selling tatty souvenirs, but there always are and they do please some people. Stratford to me was compromise at its best, compromise between the old and the new. And you've got to have the new, the car parks and amenities, you've got to have cafés and restaurants to cater for visitors, because they in fact keep the town alive. I like Stratford and I congratulate all those who have made it what it is now.

THE DEBS

WHEN I've told people that I was writing about my London Season, they said, 'What London Season? It's dead. There isn't such a thing. It went out with presentations at Court.' My reply to that has been, 'You ask the debs and their escorts, the mums and dads, their bank managers and stockbrokers. They'll tell you a different story.'

I had a number of opportunities of meeting the various people involved both at the events of the Season and at the parties I went to. Apart from the debs, it's the mums that are most nearly concerned, and they are certainly the ones who do most of the worrying.

The worrying starts the year before the daughters are to come out. First, a close look at the potential material, the daughter. Is she ready for it? Has the puppy-fat begun to disappear? (Hope she gets rid of those pimples.) Has she developed all right, socially? Will she be strong enough to stand the pace? Will she want to do it, anyway? Oh dear!

Then there's Father to be thought of. How much can he afford? Shall we give a party of our own or share one, or just give a cocktail party? Oh dear!

What about dates? Mustn't clash parties with Cynthia, Margaret, Bella, etc, etc. And we mustn't forget, we've got to go through the same thing next year when our younger daughter comes out. Oh dear!

So it goes on. Tea parties with other mums, endless discussions, and gradually the programme takes shape.

Like anything else these days it's bound to be more expensive than Dad budgeted for, so his face gets longer and longer and every feminine wile has to be practised upon him. One thing that struck me as I listened was that fundamentally people of any class or position are the same. There are the same worries and problems, and the same way round them, in organizing a deb's Season as there is for a working-class family arranging a week's holiday to Blackpool.

Tough though the planning is, according to three mums I spoke to it's nothing to what their mothers went through years ago. The operation then was handled with the precision and skill of a general launching a campaign, and the poor wretched daughter was continually made aware of what her responsibilities were and what was expected of her.

When 'D' Day came, it was as terrifying as going into battle and though there was a similar excitement, behind it was the fear of failure – the dread of not bringing off a successful, ie eligible marriage or, worse still, not having even one proposal. Apparently, proposals were considered as a notch in the butt of the matrimonial rifle, and were boasted about then and in later life as old campaigners did of their battle honours. Barbara Cartland was, according to her books, the female 'Sir Lancelot' during her Season. She got forty-nine proposals and just missed a disastrous marriage. The successful debs certainly had a wonderful time, wore marvellous clothes, went to all the most exciting parties; even though chaperoned it was possible to escape the eagle eye sometimes.

Today, although much of the planning is as arduous as it ever was, the quest for a husband is no longer the paramount aim. Some debs do find husbands but, generally speaking, they don't 'enter the arena' looking for them; nor do they have the feeling of responsibility towards their parents that they used to have. It's more a fun thing participated in with the idea of making friends, both male and female, that will last them for a number of years and see them all right socially.

The debs I spoke to confirmed this. A lot of them at the beginning had gone into the Season because their parents had wanted them to. They couldn't really see the point of it. 'After all,' as one said, 'nowadays we don't need a Season to meet men, we mix with them all the time in restaurants, clubs and pubs. And other places, too,' she added, cryptically. 'I think it's going to be a bit of a bore.'

Yet towards the end of the Season when I spoke to her again she said it hadn't really been boring. 'We did meet the same people over and over again. It was like a social merry-go-round – a sort of large-sized Paul Jones. This, though, seems to me the point of it all. You get to know well quite a few people of your own age and social group. The more you see them the better you like them and the less you want to meet people who are, as it were, outside the circle. I reckon I've met people who will be my friends for life. It's a sort of social foundation. This applies particularly to girls, the other debs. The men, well, they're not a bad lot by and large. Conversationally they're a bit limited and they're rather stereotyped in the way they try to maul you. Fending them off becomes a matter of routine. Any escort who could discover a new routine for seduction would find himself overwhelmed with party invitations.'

Another deb, while grudgingly admitting she'd enjoyed herself, said that she'd only agreed to do it to please her parents. 'As far as I can see it will be the last thing I do that will please them since I intend getting a flat next month and shacking up with my boyfriend.'

I was interested in the economics. She wasn't too sure about these. 'I suppose it's cost them about £5,000, including clothes and drinks and things. The party alone cost over £2,000. It wasn't a success either. We had to invite relations and friends from Wiltshire and Cheshire. They just stood around like country cousins. It just didn't jell,' she said. Expensive sort of jam, I thought.

She hadn't made any male friends. 'I didn't want to. I seem to prefer older men like my present boyfriend. Not that I'd have been faithful to him if I'd found anything better. I just didn't.'

I protested that this seemed like taking money from her parents under false pretences. She didn't see it that way. 'Both Mummy and Daddy had a whale of a time, and you have to pay for pleasure these days.'

Some of the debs work, often quite seriously. Sally, for instance, made leather trousers. She reckoned to make five pairs a day, at £1 a pair. Not bad for a day's work, though how she managed it keeping all those late hours I don't know. Others get an allowance. 'Daddy gives me £15 a week. I do the odd modelling job which brings me in another £10 but since we go dutch with our escorts it isn't enough. Occasionally Mummy coughs up a bit if I get into debt but she's not keen to.'

None of the girls took the business at all seriously. They realized that the Season was out of step with modern ideas and they supposed the end justified the means. There was little gratitude to their parents. 'They know what they're doing. They push us into the Season because they think it's the done thing. It gives them a certain *cachet*. Mummy, particularly. She goes to lots of lunch and tea parties with other mothers. She pretends she's bored with it all but I know she isn't. It gives her a reason for dressing up and wearing her pearls. She also relives the memories of her own Season and of her success in snaffling an eligible young man – even though she usually ends up making bitchy comparisons. Daddy, of course, is happy because Mummy's enjoying herself and is kept busy. He also likes pinching my girlfriends' bottoms. The only thing he positively hates is paying the bills.'

I'd met a few escorts at Queen Charlotte's Ball. Others I was introduced to later were more prepossessing. Some were doing their third Season and were looking forward to many more. They had no matrimonial intentions. They said they couldn't afford them. According to the debs, such escorts are absolute life-savers for the girls who can't find a partner for the evening. Many have no money, but they do have the right background and accent, and the correct clothes.

These 'debs' delights', as they are known, form a sort of male harem. Technically they are 'on the list', which is how they get their invitations to the events and parties. Officially this list is never acknowledged but it circulates privately, and places on it are hotly contested. There are some, of course, who are there by an inalienable right. Their ancestry and background are an *open sesame* to any deb's door. Others get on because they are good-looking, wear the right clothing, dance well, are charming conversationally, hold their drink and keep their noses clean. The list is vetted by a certain someone whose name is whispered deferentially by those who seek his favour and somewhat differently by those already favoured. He also has a black list of the gatecrashers, drunkards and deb-molesters. He must have a busy time keeping that up to date.

In between parties and events debs and their escorts mingle in pubs, restaurants and clubs. The clubs are rather a treat for the majority as they're very expensive. I should know, I went with a party to one. I rather expected the kind of behaviour that one reads goes on in these new pubs, or 'Birds' Nests' as they're called. People necking, giggling, and go-go girls go-going around the place. It wasn't a bit like that. All right, it was dimly lit and there was a lot of loud music but everyone seemed to be behaving with great decorum. Despite the music I was able to chat to the deb next to me. I compared my courting days with hers. It appears there are still the 'drips', as Gladys the housemaid and I used to call some of our boys, the languid ones who'd saunter over nonchalantly to ask you to dance as though they were doing you an enormous favour. If they opened their mouths it was only to come out with some inane expression. There are the mean ones who muscle in when anyone else is paying but fade away if it looks as though they have to make a contribution. There are the officers. With us it was guardsmen who were over-conscious of their appearance and talked too much about the regiment. Then of course there are the handsome and charming who everybody's after and who I never stood a chance with. They all have something in common – sex – a sort of 'What's in it for me at the end of the evening' way of behaving. Of course with me it had to end with kissing. I was too ignorant and scared to risk going any further.

But times have changed. With this deb I was chatting to it was a case of 'maybe, but only if I like to and want to'. There's now a great difference in the attitude of men towards a rebuff. In my young days they would often get into a rage and call you a waste of money and time. Now there are no protests, no hard feelings. As she said, 'There's more than one list in operation for the Season. The escorts have theirs of the girls that *do*, or *may* or *don't*.' Presumably a failed night-out with a 'may' doesn't preclude a visit to a 'do'; not in these days of fast cars.

Anyway, although I couldn't have featured on the escorts' list that night, I certainly enjoyed myself with them. I danced continuously and they were polite enough to say that they enjoyed dancing with me. They said that they had never danced in a nightclub with someone who wore a hat all the time. Well, I'd bought the hat I was wearing that afternoon; I thought it would make me look more respectable in a nightclub. When the owner came up to our table and chatted me up he didn't seem to notice the hat which was a pity as I'd paid £5 for it.

Apparently today there are 'In' and 'Out' clubs. At the moment his was very much in, but he was philosophical about it. He seemed quite prepared to find in six months' time that he was out. He said it was hard work running a club and trying to look enthusiastic about it at three o'clock in the morning. He'd be quite prepared to pack it in and try something else. Judging by the size of the bill at the end, he needn't have worried – he'd have been able to finance himself in just about anything.

More dancing, more compliments, more drink and more confidences from the debs. Once again our ideas ran parallel. Although they were enjoying their new freedom, it appeared that they ultimately wanted to get married, have children, settle down. They didn't take what we believe to be the modern line: I can try it, if I don't like it then it can easily be ended. They wanted a husband for keeps. Perhaps they just said it because they thought it was what I wanted to hear. I like to believe it was '*In vino, veritas*'. Anyway, it made me happy, so happy that I accepted the owner's invitation to take over as disc jockey for the rest of the night or, I should say, morning. I reckon that was as big a compliment as being handed the drum sticks by Harry Roy would have been in my day.

After the somewhat frenetic goings on at the nightclub I was keen to see the debs at some other form of play. My escort had got a sort of debs' pub crawl list from some of their escorts, and we set off round Belgravia, a fringe area of Chelsea. We were advised not to choose a weekend;

then the pubs get so packed it's difficult to raise a drink to your mouth. They were all busy enough even on a Monday, particularly towards the end of the evening. Our itinerary was the Prince of Wales, the Horse & Groom, and The Grenadier, in that order.

I expected that the pubs debs used would be the modern juke-box kind of place and I was surprised to find that they were all what I call real pubs. That is to say, they hadn't been tarted up. They'd been made comfortable but had retained their original character and I can't remember hearing music in any of them. They mainly had only one bar which they didn't even trouble to label 'Saloon'. Albert and I used to like pubs where the bars are divided. Saturday night we wore our best and used the saloon bar. If we could afford a drink mid-week we went into the public bar where the beer was cheaper. Nowadays you see bars labelled 'Lounge Bar'. I avoid those places. I don't like the word 'lounge' to start with, and I don't like the interpretation the brewers put on it: a sort of home from home. I go to a pub to get away from home. What's the point in exchanging one sitting-room for another? I want a complete change of atmosphere. A pub should be 'pubby'. These all were and that I think is why they were popular. They were also dramatic, the obviously rich drinking shoulder to shoulder with working-class people and engaging in conversation and banter with them.

Another thing they had in common were the landlords and ladies. A lot of people think that running a pub is a cushy life. I suppose it can be, but to run one successfully needs intelligence, discernment and discretion. I don't think you've got to be a 'character' to be a good publican. Too many try to be the centre of attraction instead of allowing their customers a measure of self-expression or the pleasure of talking among themselves. They try to run the pub for themselves and to involve themselves in their customers' lives. They have their favourites and end up turning the pub into a kind of a club. A good publican is first a strategist. He finds out the kind of pub his area requires, and caters for this. Then, a tactician: welcoming his customers, laughing and joking with them when they want his company yet disappearing into the background when they don't. Always alert and ready to move to an area where he is most needed. These were the qualities I found.

One of the landlords I spoke to, although not a young man, enjoyed catering for the youth. He was full of praise for them. Considered they were a lot more intelligent and level-headed than his generation; more socially aware and generally more purposeful. In the main I agreed with him though I do get a bit fed-up with constantly hearing that the young today are so concerned with poverty, bad housing and the aged. In my experience a lot of voluntary work for the underprivileged is done by older people, not just by the young.

It's interesting that over the last ten years young people have come back to using pubs. Before that, it was coffee bars. I asked one or two what they thought was the reason, but none could explain. They didn't reckon it was because there was more money about, nor because the brewers had wooed them back. Indeed they considered the so-called improvements and amenities in pubs off-putting.

I think young people would like to see the licensing laws relaxed, and restaurants and cafés allowed to serve drinks throughout the day. None of them seemed to want to drink to excess. They did think though that it helped in social contacts, that alcohol broke down barriers and inhibitions, and helped to create a greater degree of friendship and bonhomie. The girls were certainly fully alert to the use of drink as a means of seduction. In fact, I think they were not only more sensible than I was when I was young but more sensible than I am now – though, of course, as far as seduction and I are concerned, opportunity would be a fine thing.

When I was the same age as a deb, girls seldom went into pubs without a male escort. My friend Gladys and I went on our own once; but what with the stares of the customers and the landlady's obvious disapproval, we hastily drank a gin and departed. The only reason that we'd gone in in the first place was because we were tired of our boyfriends who were not prepared to spend more than a half-crown on the 'pictures' and a cup of tea in Lyons.

Although, like nightclubs, there are 'In' pubs and 'Out' pubs, they tend to stay 'In' for very much longer. Some have been popular over many years. This of course is understandable. Opening a pub is a very different thing from opening a club.

Debs' pubs have their sort of stage-door Johnnies. I talked with one who admitted he was on the prowl for dollies. His eyes were constantly on the alert even while he was chatting to me. He was in his late thirties and was what I would have thought young girls would have considered a dirty old man, but he boasted quite openly of his conquests. Apparently some girls like older men, particularly those who have money and a comfortable pad. He was very charming and likeable in his way, and free with his drinks, but he obviously was not going to delay his quest by talking to me for long. He made his adieu and we wished him good hunting.

Although each pub was different from the other in period and surroundings, there were mostly the same kind of customers in all of them. The exception was when we got ourselves involved with a party of bank managers who were attending some convention in London and like ourselves were surveying the young scene.

They started singing what I was told by my escort were rugger songs. All I can say is if anyone had sung them in my local in Hove they'd have been outside after a couple of verses. It was like watching a lot of schoolboys and if any of their customers had been in the bar I reckon he could have got himself a large overdraft at the price of his silence. I didn't think bank managers were like that at all.

Our last port of call, The Grenadier, was in Wilton Mews. This pub was originally an Officers' Mess and I think the Duke of Wellington was a regular customer. Of course the beer was cheaper, and stronger, at that time; it needed to be. This pub seemed livelier than the previous two, perhaps because it was a smaller place and we were crammed together. Togetherness is all where drinking is concerned.

I got talking to two or three debs in the loo – always a leveller of age and social status, especially if there is only one loo and some half-dozen would-be users, jockeying for position in the queue. A very pretty girl informed me that her parents had given her the ghastly name of Charlotte and she was doing the equally ghastly Season.

I said that I was having a marvellous time with my Season; what did she find wrong with hers?

'The whole thing's drippy. The men are drips, the parties drippy, and the functions even drippier.'

We couldn't pursue the conversation since by now she was head of the queue and a vacancy occurred. Talk about pleasing some of the people some of the time, some people you can't please any of the time. It all goes to show that the deb world is very much like other worlds, gay one minute, depressed and critical the next. It seems that no matter what you get in the way of opportunity and entertainment, it can still turn sour on you.

DINNER AT THE SAVOY

As a sort of farewell to the Season, my escort announced that he was taking me to the Savoy for dinner and I admit I got the kind of shivering thrill of excitement that Cinderella must have felt when her Fairy Godmother told her she was going to the Ball. To me, and I think to a lot of other people, the name stands for the most luxurious hotel in the world. Not that I'd been round the world; I hadn't even been to the Savoy yet. It was just the sound and feeling of the name.

So that I should know a bit about the place and what went on there, my escort gave me a brochure. I began browsing through it. The fact that it ranks with the Waldorf Astoria in New York and the Hotel de Paris in Monte Carlo meant nothing to me because, as I've said, I've been in neither, but it sort of confirmed my shiver of excitement. I wasn't particularly impressed to learn that it is an hotel much used by Americans, because what hotel isn't? Even the sort of semi-boarding-house place that Albert and I stay at when we have to spend a night in London is used by them. I know this partly because of their accents, and partly because they cut up their food, then put the knife on the side of their plates and eat with a fork.

It was when I read that the food consumed annually at the Savoy includes half a ton of fresh caviare, fourteen tons of smoked salmon and two tons of *foie gras* that I started to get worried. Surely this sort of thing was political and social dynamite, enough to start any revolutionary feeling for his gun. Such provisions could hardly be considered as the basic necessities of life.

I read on: sheets on the beds are changed every day. Well, I suppose if you've got the kind of money it needs to stay at the Savoy, it's such a worry to you that you need clean sheets every night to get off to sleep. Then, some more statistics. There is a staff of fifteen hundred to look after five hundred guests. It's like a bee-hive, isn't it, where the worker bees look after the drones? The only difference is that the drones don't get thrown out of the hive when they've fulfilled their function. From the Savoy they move of their own accord to further luxury.

Then I came to a pulsating bit of blurb: 'The Savoy is perfumed with an aura lingering from the rich and regal England of Edward VII and glittering in the approval of contemporary royalty.' My thoughts reverted to my own domestic life. I couldn't help wondering if the kitchen staff lingered in a perfumed aura. I know I used to smell of washing-up water and yellow soap the best part of the day.

The private dining-rooms are named after the Gilbert and Sullivan operas. In one of these the most exclusive dining club in Britain meets. It's called the 'Other Club'. It was founded by Winston Churchill and Lord Birkenhead. Its members are superstitious, for if there are only thirteen present a three-foot model of a black cat occupies a place and it is served with the full meal. Well, I suppose it's something that the Club hasn't got a colour bar.

That sort of chat in a brochure doesn't really endear me to a place. I start getting guilt feelings and my class-conscious blood starts to boil a bit. However, it provided me with a talking point for a few days and as a result I got some more information. Apparently, the head porter there earns more than the Prime Minister and the chief lavatory attendant sends his son to Eton. Or is it possible that some of my friends were sending me up? I must say, though, when I arrived at the Savoy with my escort and a porter opened the door of the cab I looked at him with awe and respect.

Inside, the place lived up to my expectations. The entrance hall was imposing and impressive. It seemed as busy as a railway station, with people bustling off in different directions, some to the Grill, others to the bars, the private dining-rooms, the lifts. We went through to the restaurant which did indeed have 'an aura lingering from the rich and regal England'. There were glittering chandeliers, deep carpets, lots of gold paint, and a highly polished dance floor which I later discovered rose at the push of a button like those Wurlitzer cinema organs used to. This gave everyone an uninterrupted view of the cabaret, when it was presented. We were ushered, almost glided, to our table, tucked up in our napkins by the waiter and had aperitifs in front of us in a twinkle.

Menus I always find worrying. I can never make up my mind what to eat, and I always seem to end up wishing I'd chosen what the person next to me has got. I also find my eyes wandering all the time to the prices, and sort of totting up what the meal is going to cost before I start. This is a mistake at the Savoy unless, like us, you're going to stick to the *table d'hôte* menu. We were pleased we did, for when you consider the surroundings, the kind and choice of food you get and the dancing and cabaret that's thrown in, it's cheaper than most Soho restaurants.

Eventually I decided what I wanted and our order was given. I had avocado pear with a sort of prawn filling and my escort half a dozen oysters. I felt no envy about these. Oysters have never meant anything to or done anything for me. I know the old Cockney expression, 'Oysters is amorous' and I've tried them to see, but they leave me cold. For the main course I had quails. I chose them because it's not a dish I can have any day of the week but is one which I remembered having to prepare and cook when I was in service. It's a rare taste and I think this is something you look for when you dine out. My escort had steak. All right it was a beauty and more filling than my quails but still I wasn't envious. The claret which we drank was as good as the one we'd enjoyed at Simpson's, which isn't surprising since both the Savoy and Simpson's are under the same management. We deserted the *table d'hôte* menu for our sweet course. I'd never had *crêpes suzettes*, and I wanted to try them. I also fancied the kind of *flambé* fuss that goes with them. Our waiter executed this with great panache, and the wine waiter was hot on his heels with a bottle of champagne. Frankly, I was disappointed. Give me lemon pancakes every time.

I compared the meal with the lunch I had at Simpson's. For me it didn't bear the comparison. While I couldn't find fault with the cooking or the service at the Savoy, it was too professional and too impersonal. Our waiter couldn't have been more efficient or pleasant but he was never involved with us or our meal. He talked to us but somehow the dinner never became an event, something to remember – the sort of interchange between eater and provider that I think is the essence of a good meal. It's a kind of communion of spirit and effort. Hard to explain and harder consciously to achieve.

The meal over, I was able to look around me. Those on the dance floor fascinated me with their various styles. There were elderly couples probably celebrating some anniversary dancing in the fashion of their youth. There were the young doing their particular thing with the antics of a barrow-load of monkeys. And there was the middle group trying to be with it and just looking somewhat incongruous. There was an element of the ridiculous about the whole scene.

I bucked up a bit as my attention was caught by the people at a table nearby where a young girl was being given a twenty-first birthday party by her father and mother. Everyone was determined to enjoy themselves and the birthday girl was obviously in raptures. A special cake was carried to the table and the band played 'Happy Birthday'.

Inevitably, I compared her state to mine when I had my twenty-first. I was taken by my parents to the local pub. It was a travesty of any evening. I didn't know how I was expected to behave and my mother had invited a young man who she thought would make me a good husband. We loathed each other on sight. As the drink flowed, more and more remarks were thrown around as to what an ideal couple we'd make. Nobody seemed to realize the embarrassment they were causing us. I was mortified, and it quite spoiled my birthday. A far cry from this happy party at the Savoy.

Towards the end of our meal our waiter told me that such is the prestige of being employed at the Savoy that staff can get a good job anywhere by just mentioning that they have worked at the hotel, never mind in what capacity; in fact one of the kitchen-porters had just got a job as an hotel manager in Spain. I didn't know whether that was any recommendation. I'd just heard from a friend of mine who was in Spain for a holiday, describing how her hotel was so badly run. The cups were chipped, the food was always late and the tea was like monkey's – well, not milk! I certainly hoped it wasn't the same hotel.

Perhaps it was because I'd expected so much from the Savoy that it didn't quite rise to my expectations. The fault was probably in me. The ingredients for a wonderful evening were all there, certainly, but something must have gone wrong in the mixing of them. I enjoyed myself but I didn't quite have the ball I'd expected. Perhaps I shouldn't have read that brochure.

So my Season is over. Some of it puzzled and confounded me; it was often tiring both to the mind and on the feet. A lot of it was exciting; none of it was boring.

All in all I had a marvellous time. I think I probably enjoyed it more than the debs. Although I knew I was going to have to write about it, I never consciously felt as though I was someone on the outside looking in. I always felt part of it. I, as it were, suspended time and age.

Although, because I was writing about it, I might have asked for some special privileges, I didn't. I went as an ordinary person, paying my own way as anybody else would have to. I think, therefore, I saw the true scene and when at times I found myself criticizing it I didn't feel I was betraying anyone's hospitality.

I am grateful to all the organizers for the way the London Season is presented, and to all the people I chatted with who helped to make it so much fun.

Margaret Powell

BELOW STAIRS 25p

'Shrewd, unabashed, wickedly funny, she gives here a unique front-line report of her life's experience in the underprivileged world of someone else's kitchen.' – JACK DE MANIO, BBC

CLIMBING THE STAIRS 25p

'Delightfully down-to-earth and always brimming with vitality.' – SUNDAY EXPRESS

THE TREASURE UPSTAIRS 30p

'Mrs. Powell goes irrepressibly on with her memories of high jinks below stairs' – EVENING STANDARD

THE MARGARET POWELL COOKERY BOOK 35p

SWEETMAKING FOR CHILDREN 20p